MAKE

WORLDS

Aykhan AtaSak

ETHNIDNATISM: THE ROAD TO SPIRITUALITY

© 2023 **Europe Books**| London
www.europebooks.co.uk | info@europebooks.co.uk

ISBN 9791220143745
First edition: October 2023
Translated by Zeynab Salamova
Editing: Edward Sheldon

ETHNIDNATISM: THE ROAD TO SPIRITUALITY

Dedication

I, Aykhan Atasak, dedicate my first book "Ethnidnatism" (The Road to Spirituality), to the Azerbaijani people and Azerbaijani ethnidnatism! The tolerance of the Azerbaijani people, their colorful ethnidnatic spirit, the peace-loving nature have made a significant contribution to the creation of this work. I pay tribute to my people who inspired me and wish them eternal happiness...

Mankind Manifestation

I intend and promise never to use the enlightenment, power, and benefits of Ethnidnatism against humanity and nature. Otherwise, let my values, beliefs, and conscience punish me. Let Ethnidnatism ensure peace among all the values that humanity has. May mankind become wiser, kinder, and more supreme with this stream, which is the key to evolution.

INTRODUCTION

We were driven into a deeper gap without knowing our demands. The internationalized demands of the modern age have become the demands of all of us. We have believed that we should all have luxury homes, cars, fashionable clothes, and a "standard" lifestyle. However, we did not ask, "Do we really need all this?" Of course, constant development of living conditions and well-being of people is wonderful, but sometimes we do not realize that to be happy we depend on material condition rather than improving our well-being.

We build houses that we will never live in, we collect cars that we will never drive, we spend lots of money on clothes that are much more expensive than their real value, but in the end, do they lead us to happiness? The answer is probably the same for many people: of course, our happiness last for a while, until we realize that those objects are accessible. After that we want more to be happier, and we have the same experience. Our material wealth makes us happy, but it lasts until we have it. The feeling of possession fascinates us so much that we are confident this image will always delight us.

A man sacrifices all his energy, time, and morality, which is his most valuable asset, to all these throughout his life. The hustle and bustle of life confuses him so much that he doesn't even have time to think. The desire to always own more drives him away from the truth. The awakened brain begins to think about it either in old age, or when it is sick and tired of getting everything. If one of the two does not happen, the period of anxiety and unhappiness follows him until the end of his life. Sometimes it's too late, and the feeling of regret and not being able to meet the demands of life make people disappointed. The man does not become disappointed materially, it is the soul of a man that constantly screams from the depths of chaotic state. The feelings of anxiety and compulsion control our lives.

Compulsion is a set of obstacles created by our brain. As the soul is free, it is not compelled to do anything. Our duty in life is to nourish our spirit and to ensure its development without suffering. Ethnidnatism has come out from the depths of life to save the souls struggling in a state of chaos. It has appeared to declare to people that the claim of possession is not on material objects, but on spiritual life.

A human being has taken many steps to protect his values and spiritual development since artificiality began to occupy human lives. However, all the methods did not help in case of "compulsion". Ethnidnatism, on the other hand, has led humanity with the most authoritative ways of explaining the phenomenon of the "ethnidnatic spirit." People will now live happier, more honestly, richer, and more spiritually with the preachments of ethnidnatism. They will appropriately use the resources of the world and will think about the welfare of future souls. In brief, man will have higher values and more easily restore peace with ethnidnatism.

The book deals with higher morality, spiritual practice, mysticism, philosophy, and many ideological currents. Thanks to this collection, "ethnidnatism - a part of the truth sought", will make the search for truth even easier. Now the mystery we are looking for everywhere will come to us as ethnidnatism. This work deals with only the simple principles, origins, and spheres of influence of ethnidnatism covered in 17 topics.

WHAT CAUSED THE EMERGENCE OF ETHNIDNATISM

Man has looked for shelter throughout the history of mankind. Each shelter sought had its own characteristic features. Having had material support at first, mankind realized there was a gap and how important the shelter, that is asylum was from a spiritual point of view. Spiritual asylums were sometimes thought to be caves at the top, sometimes a rooted tree, and even a rock thought to be sacred. Confidence in every moment of fear, preparation before going hunting, protection from invasions and attacks, was a phenomenon of spiritual asylum rather than material support.

Spiritual asylums were the source of people's strength, the secret of their success, the philosophy of their life. It was the source of deep faith, the driving force behind all success. Spiritual asylums began to take shape over the centuries, even turning into magnificent temples. This revolution was reflected not only in the spiritual world, but also in the physical world. As a result, shelters have left great mark on the history of mankind.

What about the "temples" built inside? As the temples built inside were subjectively perceived, they were never recorded in history, but always preserved in spiritual values. Objective temples originated from shelters, but what were the subjective temples built inside?

The temples built inside were a system of beliefs taught to people and formed in them. These temples were considered so powerful and sophisticated that some masters, shamans, or sage people constantly taught and preached them. This system of beliefs had different forms in every society, in every geography, in every continent.

In spite of their different forms, every human being was committed to belief and value with great sympathy and faith. It was due to the soul they possessed which always gave them strength and made up a large part of their daily lives. They associated their food, physical strength, and achievements with that strength.

What was the secret of strength? Is there still such force today? The secret of strength was in deep beliefs and feelings. The potential energy of the human body is so strong that the events that seem legendary for us today were known in the past as real. Due to the power of feelings and faith, the physical body became more tolerant than usual. There are millions of people who have experienced this and are still living today.

The point here is not that faith gives strength, but what it relies on. There is a common foundation on which all human beings are endowed by beliefs. This foundation is the "ethnidnatic spirit." Ethnidnatic spirits are secret feelings-secret temples that people feel inside but have not been able to reveal for centuries. It is as if human instinct wanted this temple to be hidden for thousands of years and always protected it with great sensitivity. In ancient times, the sages who did great things with the help of such an "ethnidnatic spirit" did not reveal it by any definition.

No matter what people believe, the power of ethnidnatic spirits has always saved people in their difficult times. Ethnidnatic spirits accompanied people in wars, were together with them in great revolutions and helped to increase their creativity. Mankind became much more colorful with ethnidnatic spirits and expressed their love through them. The common feature that united people apart from the physical factors was the nature of the ethnidnatic spirits. Today, ethnidnatic spirits are strengthened by the civil ties of the international community, but on the one hand, the number of people with an ethnidnatic spirit is decreasing.

Ethnidnatism is the art of revealing and encouraging the development of ethnidnatic spirits within. Every human being who knows and lives by the simple principles of ethnidnatism has a more creative, high-qualitative, original, and happier life. It is because ethnidnatism can regard unknown as known one.

FUNDAMENTALS OF ETHNIDNATISM

The word **ethnidnatism** is a combination of 3 words derived from the ancient Latin language. The name was chosen in Latin to make it easier for everyone to understand, as Latin is the language of philosophy and international terms. These three words are:

"Ethnos" means culture, ethnicity, nation, a group of people living as a tribe.
"Ideo" means thought, idea, logic.
"Natio" means nation, tribe, generation, family.

Ethnidnatism is a philosophical movement that embodies multicultural, cosmopolitan, national, and ethnic values and believes that there is an essence hidden in every thought, philosophy, ideology, and nationality. It is a philosophy that teaches to find out this essence. Ethnidnatism, contrary to all racist ideas, believes that there is an essence of peace in every ideology. According to ethnidnatism, negativity is impossible when there is philosophy and ideas. If an idea seems negative, then there are individuals who hide it in a negative way. The world is colored by ethnos, nations, and the ideologies they create. Therefore, ethnidnatism considers each of them as a color of the world.

According to ethnidnatism, not only logic and perception, but also the spirit and morality of that thought play an important role in any thought. Therefore, ethnidnatism divides the spirit of human thought, which is the color of the world, into three parts. It is possible to live and feel these spirits at the same time and separately. These 3 parts are:

Ethnic spirit is a type of spirit that belongs to a form of an ethnos not mixed with other cultures. In order to experience the ethnic spirit, it is necessary to reveal the philosophies of the tribes lived in history and the essence of those philosophies.

Ideological spirit is a spirit formed from an ideological way of thinking. We can give as an example religious, philosophical, sociological, mystical, and individual spirits.

National spirit is a name given to a spirit that combines the spiritual essence of more than one different or similar ethnos and ideology. The spirit created by many states or nations in the world is an example of it.

For centuries, people mocked at each other's spiritual way of thinking, but they failed to realize that ethnidnatic spirit stood in the center of every thought. The fear of such mockery prevented the emergence of many ethnidnatic spirits. These obstacles led to the disappearance of many ethnidnatic spirits that existed for some time.

Unfortunately, the same process is going on nowadays. The concept of ethnidnatism will be a new life and soul for the disappearing ethnidnatic spirits. Therefore, ethnidnatism promotes the philosophy of being able to live every ethnidnatic spirit. It is necessary for people to understand one other and develop empathy. This is the only way to ensure peace in the world.

Ethnidnatism is the art of being able to perceive every existing ethnidnatic spirit like the individual who experiences that spirit.

There is a necessity to follow the principles of any way of thinking in order to bear the name. In ethnidnatism, however, every human being is an ethnidnatist, because every human being has an ethnidnatic spirit. An ethnidnatist who realizes that he has an ethnidnatic spirit should never mock at the ethnidnatic spirit of others. No matter how far away that spirit is, he must realize the essence of that spirit and understand the person in front of him through empathy. This process is called to live by the spirit in an ethnidnatic way.

Future generations who understand the simple concepts we have described so far will be able to live more peacefully and wisely in the world. Those who comprehend ethnidnatism are ultimately considered ethnidnatists. Ethnidnatism describes the true ethnidnatists as follows: they are a Bedouin Arabic in the desert, a Shintoist in a pagoda, a Masai in Africa, and a Mayan in the Amazon. True ethnidnatists can easily live up to these spirits and try the essence of each ethnidnatic spirit of different colors, which are not related to one other.

They use the mirror theorem to reach the essence of ethnidnatic spirit. By this theorem they perceive the spirit and reflect it externally through fables. Of course, there is no rule that the experienced ethnidnatic spirits must be lived up to throughout the life. It is due to the fact that ethnidnatic spirit is free and exists in accordance with human ego. In reality, however, there is one or more ethnidnatic spirits close to each of us, which can be more easily united with our ego. This ethnidnatic spirit is considered to be the spirit we possess and constantly develop through practice.

The greatest benefit of ethnidnatism for mankind is to have a deep spirituality, to understand people more easily, and to look at life philosophically and with pleasure. Ethnidnatism is influential not only in the development of people's spiritual aspects, but also in the development of their mental aspects. People who practice ethnidnatism tend to think more creatively, more analytically and correctly in every field. This is because they can look at the world with different eyes. The more people look at the world, the more active become their brains. The natural energy flow in the brain is further accelerated and leads to an increase in hormones of happiness. As we mentioned in the first subject, man sees his soul as a refuge because it is coded to seek refuge. This refuge gives him confidence in many fields.

HOW TO UNDERSTAND ETHNIDNATISM?

Each of us has empathized at least once in our lives to be born in another life. Whether we are satisfied with our present life or not, we are always interested in different lives. Ethnidnatism is a small journey into the lives of others, because we can never understand the essence of ethnidnatism if we do not travel imaginatively into the lives of others. For this reason, "imagination" is always one of the most important tools in understanding ethnidnatism.

The image of Bedouin ethnidna environment

Let's take a small journey to understand ethnidnatism: imagine you were born in a tent on the Arabian Peninsula, among the Bedouins. All that you see around is the sand and camels, and you speak a language that is difficult for other nations. Every day you work on the traditions of the desert people and keep in touch with them.

Don't forget that you possess as much as they have, because that's the most important part of the imagination. Imagine a holiday or a wedding in the desert. The ceremony, which takes place in luxurious palaces in ordinary cities, is held in the desert with a group of people gathered around the fire, with their music and dances. Accept with all your heart that this is your home. Imagine what we have said so far right now ... Now wake up, it's time to analyze. The desert and the Arab-Bedouin ethnidnatic spirit formed in the desert, where you traveled for a moment is just one of the millions of ethnidnatic spirits that have emerged in the world.

There are millions of people born and raised in real life in that environment that you imagine for a moment. Naturally, the Arab-Bedouin ethnidnatic spirit is formed in these people as well. In ethnidnatism this formation is called the **ethnidnatic spirit created by the environment.** The factors such as nationality, landscape, climate, language, religion, customs, mentality, way of thinking have formed your ethnidnatic spirit in compliance with the place where you were born. You may not enjoy Indian music, customs and traditions, or French art as much as your own culture, but you will easily be able to live up with other ethnidnatic spirits that are close to your spirit. Even observations prove that Arabs, who grew up in high-rise buildings in urban environments, no matter how much they love the urban environment, enjoy tents, deserts, and other objects of that environment more and these objects give them a deeper spiritual pleasure. As a result, we can say that the ethnidnatic spirit of each individual is, first of all, associated with the environment in which he was born.

The opposite of all the mentioned before is also possible. For example, imagine that you were born in a noble English family in England, but in English culture you can never find the peace, spiritual pleasure, love, and harmony which you find in Indian culture. This is called *the journey of ethnidnatic spirit.* Because the ego inside has formed in Indian ethnidnatism. Thus, a person has defined his ethnidnatic spirit through small trips. These trips can be ordinary TV show today. In other words, there is no need for the person we are talking about to go to India, because he has mastered his ethnidnatic spirit with a small understanding and satisfied his own spiritual taste. Sometimes in our real life we love the culture we have never seen and have nothing to do with it. We want to be a part of that culture for a moment, and we can feel inside that we are part of them. This is the best example of *the journey of the ethnidnatic spirit.*

It is a pity that millions of people around the world are born in big cities apart from their ethnidnatic spirits. People who do not have ethnidnatic spirit first tend to depression and then suicide, because they are far from the colors, passion and meaning of life. In ethnidnatism it is called ethnidnatic deficiency syndrome. This syndrome, which is even not understood by many psychologists, is formed subconsciously and develops over the years. When no cure is found for the syndrome, sedative antidepressants are tried, but in most cases this treatment does not work.

The first sign of *ethnidnatic deficiency syndrome* is the inability to identify oneself. That is, not being able to find out who he is and why he lives. This leads to the lack of purpose. Aimlessness can have a negative impact on social life, work life and family life.

Another sign is the feeling of not being loved, of being useless to humanity and the world. Man is not nourished spiritually, because he cannot find the ethnidnatic environment to which he belongs. Spiritually malnourished souls and brains are doomed to death. Thus, the symptoms of the syndrome overlap, leading to depression and suicide. We will talk in more detail about ethnidnatic deficiency syndrome and other issues in Ethnidnatic Psychology.

The matter is quite different for people who have discovered their ethnidnatic spirit. Although life is full of difficulties for them, they are happy because they do not try to be happy by making their lives alike to the lives of others. As individuals, they create their own morality in an unprecedented way. They reveal the secret of happiness hidden in the depths of life only with their spirituality. According to ethnidnatism, each person is a source of infinity, where consciousness and spirit are united. This is because every person has his own essence, thinking and morality. Every person has his own irreplaceable ethnidnatic spirit.

This doctrine of ethnidnatism for mankind will help people to live a more secure, peaceful, and prosperous life. Because ethnidnatism has nothing to do with politics, radicalism, grouping and other non-philosophical issues. Ethnidnatism is a philosophy, thinking and spirituality.

ETHNIDNATIC UPLIFT

The formation of energetic excitement and pleasure in body in a spiritually inclined environment is called the Ethnidnatic Uplift of Spirit.

Let's explain the ethnidnatic uplift in detail: Suppose a person always lives up with the ethnidnatic spirit of an Italian state of the Middle Ages. Thus, this person eagerly visits the places belonging to that ethnidnatic spirit and nourishes his spirit in this direction. He enters a castle (museum) of that period, he takes special pleasure in every moment of the exhibits, jewelry, and architectural structure there. Sometimes, in the place that is in harmony with his spirit, his pleasure is so deep that it activates all kinds of emotions completely and simultaneously.

In an instant, a person feels more than one close but different emotions at a time, such as euphoria, pride, or excitement. These emotions are so strong that, for a moment, one can feel that the ground was cut under his feet. All this does not happen for no reason, it is caused by the rising of the ethnidnatic spirit close to it. In short, this vibration is called "ethnidnatic uplift".

An unknown image of ethnidnatic uplift

We can show the spirit of patriotism as a true example to it. The spirit instilled in societies as the spirit of patriotism is a kind of ethnidnatic spirit. Because when we talk about patriotism, an existing spirit that forms the same harmony as the environment, nationality, ideology, etc. of that country is represented. All the items from their music to their clothes support the same ethnidnatic spirit. Anthems and marches are usually considered the peak of the patriotic spirit, that is, of national ethnidnatism. All individuals who identify themselves with that country experience an ethnidnatic uplift when they hear the anthem. The individual feels that he is a part and a spirit of that society. As a result, you feel a sense of pride, excitement, pride, and a special vibration when you hear only your anthem. Of course, it is a little difficult for a representative of another nation to feel this uplift. This is because he has never experienced the ethnidnatic spirit taught to you and to your society. In order to understand that spirit, he must at least live in the same environment as you and form that spirit inside. In conclusion, not every individual can experience the same ethnidnatic uplift to the same extent. Ethnidnatic spirits formed within people vary according to environments, experiences, and practices.

FREEDOMS AND RESTRICTIONS IN ETHNIDNATISM

Ethnidnatism is the art of revealing the essence within people. Every human has an essence being unaware of it. According to ethnidnatism, this essence is the ethnidnatic spirit that belongs to him as a person. In most cases public fear often prevents ethnidnatic spirits from being detected. People hide their ethnidnatic spirits for the rest of their lives to avoid being criticized. In some societies, the ethnidnatic spirit has become the norm. This is a law the violation of which can even lead to death. There are even ethnidnatic migrants in the world who migrate to other countries simply because they cannot live up with the spirit they want in their society.

In most developed countries of the world this fear of society is thought to have disappeared. Thus, people in those countries can openly express their ethnidnatic spirit. If necessary, they create the environment they want in their own countries or organize trips to other countries.

In ethnidnatism the development and progress of the soul is possible only through propaganda. Propaganda ensures the freedom of the inner aura. Free aura leads to the growth and strengthening of the soul. A strong spirit means a healthy body and a productive life. A sound *soul* dwells within a sound mind and a *sound body.* Non-propagated ethnidnatic spirit, on the other hand, never develops, even it disappears in the darkness of the inner world.

The concept of ethnidnatism, observing all these processes, refers to the process of development of ethnidnatic spirits by two theorems.

These theorems contradict to each other. They are: *freedoms and restrictions.*

In ethnidnatism, the restriction of the ethnidnatic spirit is the propaganda of ethnidnatic spirit which is hindered for certain reasons.

The short term for this theorem is called *restrictions.* Billions of people live in different environments around the world. Billions of people are the indicators of the existence of millions of identical or different ethnidnatic groups. Within this existence, one issue is relevant to ethnidnatism, that is: the majority most people live a life different from their ethnidnatic spirits. The biggest factor in being different is the fear of society. Fears vary from society to society, but the most common fear is condemnation for being different.

For example, one person has an ethnidnatic spirit of Tibetan Buddhism, but he lives is Latin America and is surrounded by this environment. Culture, understanding, religion, language, and mentality in Latin America are completely different from those in Tibet. Therefore, a person with such a different ethnidnatic spirit cannot live up with his own way of life, his own ethnidnatic spirit. Living standards are also among the influencing factors, but the general way of thinking in society often outweighs the living standards. This person always cares about the thoughts of others, and he has the fear of being alienated from society and his being different from the ethnidnatic spirit of the place. Since he understands that the reason why he cannot live his inner soul freely is the society, he does not try to live up with the ethnidnatic spirit he possesses. As a result, his inner spirit is doomed to destruction. We have already talked about the consequences of the ethnidnatic spirits condemned to destruction.

Another obstacle to restricted spirits is the notion of fashion formed in the world. Our concept of fashion is inspecting our spirits forcibly like Cinderella's sisters trying her shoes. Putting ethnidnatic spirits in fashion prevents our spirit from developing. We, who are not visible like the point on the map of the world, are proud to force our spirits into the fashion mold. Instead of nurturing our ethnidnatic spirit and becoming a positive person, we nurture our egos and turn into rude monsters. In fact, fashion is the promotion of a free spirit. The most beautiful expression of the ethnidnatic spirit is fashion. Just as not everyone has the same ethnidnatic spirit, it is impossible for everyone to be in the same fashion. If we wear clothes and listen to music just to please others, then we become slaves of others for their understanding. We, who have become slaves in order to please the others, add our ego to it. The only reality is the ethnidnatic spirit that shouts "save me" inside a person. The restriction of the ethnidnatic spirit by such a general notion is nothing but the torment that man inflicts on his own spirituality.

Let's look at this matter differently: wearing clothes that fit our ethnidnatic spirit is more comfortable and positive for us than clothes that are fashionable. Every time when we dress and listen to music that suits our ethnidnatic spirit, we become closer to who we are. Our ethnidnatic spirit is our identity. People who do not know who they are cannot be happy. Though their closets are always full, they are not happy. They can't find a place for their shoes, but they are still looking for shoes. Every year new "hit" songs are released and forgotten, because they do not nourish the ethnidnatic spirit of the people, but rather limit it.

Choosing clothes that suit our ethnidnatic spirit will both prevent from waste and make us happy with what we wear. Natural resources are not inexhaustible, so much wasted resources are only the beginning of the doomsday created for us by common fashion. Music close to ethnidnatic spirit provides silence and thought. The notion of fashionable music is only the result of selfish instruction. According to ethnidnatism, selfishness and hatred are not right things in the propagation of the ethnidnatic spirit, because the ethnidnatic spirit, which is our identity and essence, can never be negative.

The unimpeded propagation of the ethnidnatic spirit is called freedom.

To live a life up with one's own ethnidnatic spirit is to freely propagate his ethnidnatic spirit. The absence of external obstacles, or preaching without seeing obstacles, is like the soul released from a bird's cage. Releasing the spirit that we propagate will be reflected on the development of spirit in our daily life. If you don't feel happy when you wake up, it is caused by external incompatibility that has arisen in the depths of your soul. The soul suffers because it knows that you will not experience the ethnidnatism that belongs to your identity, that you will not dress in accordance with your spirit. On the contrary, a person with the appearance and way of life in accordance with the ethnidnatic spirit starts the day with great enthusiasm, and wants to restore the nourishment of the soul, which remained passive during sleep. People who release the ethnidnatic spirit are not obliged to prove themselves on social networks because they live a full and meaningful life. This is because their way of life has already been proved by preaching. In this way, he spends the time he wastes in virtual life for the development of his life and society. He feels that he is a part of the society with benefits he gives to it.

The freedoms are not always so easy as they seem. As we mentioned above, some societies are a great barrier to free existence of ethnidnatic spirits. People living in such societies can also get free preaching only in one way. This way is to do favor with the ethnidnatic spirit to which they belong. Notions such as charity and kindness are a form of behavior that is accepted in all societies. If anyone interferes with the spirit you preach, treat them kindly. Favor to some people is not proved once and for all but understood only after it has been done many times. If such people try to hinder you again even after your goodness, they will be confronted either with conscience or society. If the obstacles are only condemnation and ridicule, then your kindness will make your ethnidnatic spirit laugh at them wisely. Because you are closer to your own identity than they are to their own identity. You are true.

THE SEARCH FOR ETHNIDNATIC SPIRIT

Every human being has two main spirits. The first spirit is his ego. Ego is considered to be the spirit that gives life to the body. In short, the source of energy in the body that we point to with our hands is "I, me". The concept of body is like a box made up of proteins and other substances. In fact, the source of our actions, our ability to cause something depends on the consciousness of this spirit. Consciousness is formed in accordance with the form of energy flow. Brain is the part where consciousness and energy flow are most active. Ego is the same in most people in terms of function and functioning. And what makes people different?

It is the ethnidnatic spirit that differs people from one another. The ethnidnatic spirit is like an outfit worn by ego. Ethnidnatism changes according to genetics, environment, national identity, ideological practice and distinguishes people from each other. This image is distinguished not only by its color and features, but also by the fact that it nourishes ego. That is why the ego needs the right influence of the environment and environmental factors to nourish the soul. The right effect also helps maintain energy balance in the body. The wrong effect disturbs the spirit, that is, the energy balance in the body.

Finding the right ethnidnatic spirit is to nourish ego properly. Ethnidnatism recommends people *to seek the ethnidnatic spirit* in order to find the right ethnidnatic spirit. Sometimes we can easily find our own ethnidnatic spirit by analyzing our tastes and desires without going too far.

In the topic of "Freedoms and Restrictions" we have mentioned that they people bound their ethnidnatic spirits. The fact is that most of them do not know what an ethnidnatic spirit is and are not seeking an ethnidnatic spirit. In short, the ethnidnatic spirit is limited by ignorance. The reason why millions of people do not achieve happiness is that they do not seek their ethnidnatic souls for the rest of their lives. The hectic work schedule and certain problems prevent them from examining what their ethnidnatic spirits are. But how can we find our ethnidnatic spirit?

In order to pursue an ethnidnatic spirit, you must first have free time even for a while. You can estimate the time spent on public transport on the way home from work on a normal working day. You can also do preliminary research in search of the ethnidnatic spirit. As part of your research, even the image of a small tribe that existed in history can help you in your search for an ethnidnatic spirit. You can make a wide range of researches in areas such as music, art, architecture and more. Therefore, research is important at the initial stage of the search.

In the second stage you must think about which ethnidnatic spirit gives you pleasure and at what point in your life. You should observe it by looking back at your past. For example, the Spanish music played on guitar by a street musician on the road has risen your ethnidnatic spirit. So, you have found out that you enjoy Spanish movies and national costumes more. That is your discovery, you have a Spanish ethnidnatic spirit. Ethnidnatic spirits exist not only in nations, but also in millions of ideologies, sects, religions, languages, ethnos and even individuals. For example, people like Fidel Castro himself, his pride, and the ethnidnatic spirit that belongs to him. In doing so, they enjoy being a personality like him. It can also be considered an ethnidnatic spirit.

The search for an ethnidnatic spirit can last for years, no one but only you can find out who you are. All you have to do is to make decisions of your own life, do not have the wrong ethnidnatic spirit. An ethnidnatic spirit that is accepted under the influence of others is called *an artificial ethnidnatic spirit.*

Artificial ethnidnatic spirits are formed of human inclinations toward others. For example, "My friend has such kind of ethnidnatic spirit, this spirit is more popular and attractive, so I have to be like that." The happiness of people under such influence lasts until they realize that their identity is not in fact the spirit they imitate.

MONO-ETHNIDNATIC SPIRITS AND
MULTI-ETHNIDNATIC SPIRITS

One of the most common problems in the search for ethnidnatic spirits is the inability to decide what an ethnidnatic spirit is. At the moment of decision, people think that they have a chance to choose only one ethnidnatic spirit. Of course, it is not true. As the concept of spirit is a free superstition, people can make as many choices as they want. Therefore, according to the perception of ethnidnatism by an individual it is divided into two parts: "mono-ethnidnatic spirits and multi-ethnidnatic spirits."

The satisfaction of an individual with one ethnidnatic spirit is called belonging to a mono-ethnidnatic spirit.

If a person prefers to live up with the ethnidnatic spirit of his choice for the rest of his life and realizes ethnidnatic uplift in this way, he is considered a mono-ethnidnatist. Mono-ethnidnatists are people who have more accurate and quick programming of mental practices and lifestyles. They have become professionals in their ethnidnatism by constantly experiencing and practicing only one ethnidnatic spirit. Despite all this, the practice of other ethnidnatic spirits by mono-ethnidnatists at short intervals cannot influence their mono-ethnidnatism, on the contrary, they can discover new paths of their own spirits.

When an individual practices more than one ethnidnatic spirit at certain intervals, it is called having a multi-ethnidnatic spirit.

Individuals with a multi-ethnidnatic spirit can live the ethnidnatic spirits of their choice together or separately at different time intervals. For example, nothing can prevent you from experiencing a Renaissance ethnidnatic spirit one day and a Celtic spirit the next. No matter how contradictory these may seem to others, they both belong to you. Ethnidnatism is a philosophy which states that human qualities and goodness are further strengthened by ethnidnatic spirits. People of different ethnidnatic backgrounds, living in the same life, are more analytical, empathetic, and able to look at life from different angles. Because they have the morality of more than one person. They also experience ethnidnatic uplift most.

Everyone, regardless of being mono or multi-ethnidnatist, must respect the ethnidnatic spirits of others and maintain human peace.

ANALYSIS OF MATERIAL OBJECTS IN ETHNIDNATISM

Ethnidnatism is a form which unites reality, philosophy, and mysticism in one teaching. People with realistic mind, those who seek philosophy, and those who are looking for mysticism will find what they are looking for with this teaching. It is enough to know what your existence needs...

Anyone with these conflicting aspects can get what is important for them from the mentioned. In ethnidnatism, the topic of "analysis of material objects" is useful for a person who analyzes it from all three aspects. This topic deals with things and objects that affect our lives. Every day we encounter these objects in our daily lives, in nature, in public places. We use some of them as technological devices, some for their function, and some for decorative purposes only. Are there any other effects of these inanimate objects on our lives besides technical ones?

We are all aware that technological devices emit radiation, but very few people pay attention to the effects of non-technological objects. In fact, everything has an energy field. All scientific disciplines confirm that things have a certain energy field. Over the years, man has become so addicted to the technology he uses that he almost forgets his mental sensitivity. The problem is that the idea of how these objects, the energy of which is confirmed by scientific fields, will affect human life is not widespread. In ethnidnatism, this issue is considered one of the priorities. Just as in the past, things played a big role in the life of our grandparents.

Ethnidnatism studies not only the scale of the impact of objects that affect human life, but also their relevance to human life. Because everyone with an ethnidnatic spirit can be negatively or positively affected by the objects and things he owns. The sofa in our living room and the table we bought for the kitchen have more impact on our lives than we can imagine. The bigger the size of objects is, the more is its impact. However, it is possible for a small object to have much larger, more powerful force.

All objects and things are produced by nature. Ethnidnatic spirits, like objects come from nature and its shades. As a result, each object belongs to certain ethnidnatic spirit. Things and objects that fit our ethnidnatic spirit force us to succeed, but objects and things that are not in harmony with our ethnidnatic spirit force us to fail, the cause of which we never know. Our house where we spend most of our time does not satisfy us spiritually and subconsciously. Although we rest physically in the house where we live, we are always mentally tired and malnourished. Malnourished, hungry soul can never bring success, creativity, and happiness to its owner.

In modern world, very few people have houses, environments, and possessions that fit their ethnidnatic spirit. That is why very few people hold the key to happiness. If you want to achieve success, creativity, and happiness, you must start from home. It doesn't matter how many square meters the house is, the important thing is that you can experience joy every time you enter there. Unfortunately, the ethnidnatic spirit cannot be found in many objects and things. This is because we can no longer find the spirit of Mother Nature, the creator of ethnidnatic spirits, in objects.

After reading these articles, let's not ruin the natural resources in order to satisfy the spirits. On the contrary, let us cultivate it so that the nature can resurrect us, because only it can give life to the dead again. We simply need to look if there is ethnidnatic spirit in the things we choose and use. We must choose the one that suits our spirit among the things that have an ethnidnatic spirit. How can we determine the existence of ethnidnatic spirit and its suitability for us?

First of all, find out the environment where your ethnidnatic spirit originated. Ethnidnatic spirits are usually formed by referring to the environment in which they first appeared. For example, it would not be right for a person of Indonesian ethnidnatism to decorate his house with Roman columns. When using decor and item, it would be more appropriate to use materials related to the local nature of Indonesia.

Objects related to Egyptian ethnidnatism

The next step is the use of original materials to nurture a clearly dominant ethnidnatic spirit. Let's explain it with examples. For example, we often come across items made of artificial products to express Egyptian ethnidnatism. Although these items express ethnidnatic spirit in form and color, they must be considered incomplete because they do not carry the ethnidnatic spirit as material. A person who wants to experience this ethnidnatic spirit may not find the same materials in Egypt, but it is enough to use the original materials in the country where he lives. He will be satisfied with the fact that the materials in the country where he lives are included in the forms of Egyptian ethnidnatism.

No matter how difficult to find original materials for people living in the city is, it is possible to produce them. As an example, we can show bamboo. Bamboo is a material widely used in the ethnidnatism of all Southeastern Asia. Bamboo production is not difficult. Items made of bamboo can nourish the ethnidnatic spirit of millions of people.

Of course, it will not be possible to prevent fake sales which claim to have ethnidnatic spirit in these materials. Many natural, but not entirely ethnidnatic materials will be sold in various ways as belonging to the ancient and ethnidnatic spirit. I want to tell every reader to take home the materials, the originality of which they are confident. If you don't reveal that the things that make your spirituality are fake for a certain period of time, it will give you a spiritual void. You will have to pay twice to replace it.

Most of the newly produced materials have *a low level of ethnidnatism*. The level of ethnidnatic spirit measures the spirit of nature and the ethnidnatic spirit in the material. Items of this amount are explored more professionally. The scale of the level of ethnidnatic spirit and the order of its detection were determined by ethnidnatic experts. This scale is measured with a range of 0-100 percentages.

The reason for the low level of ethnidnatic spirit in newly produced materials is related to the functional aspect of the materials. The people who make the material only calculate what it will fit physically. Ethnidnatism, on the other hand, seeks the ethnidnatic spirit in material as it views it not only physically but also spiritually. But why is it impossible to find the spirit of nature or the ethnidnatic spirit in materials in so many things and objects produced?

The artificiality of the material produced and its adaptation to artificial fashion lose the spirit of nature in them. It is the person himself who gives the ethnidnatic spirit to the materials. If there is little human factor in the production of a material, it is impossible for an object made of that material to have the spirit of nature and the ethnidnatic spirit. Materials made by robots and machines must be considered dead. Because the technique that kills them cannot give those materials an ethnidnatic spirit again like a human being. Therefore, handicrafts, any objects made by artists adding their own spirits are more valuable.

Craftsmen instill an ethnidnatic spirit in every work they create. Each blow with a hammer and chisel adds a new spirit to the work. The material cut on the machines is only functionally dead. As each environment instills its own ethnidnatic spirit in the craftsman, the craftsman in his turn transfers his ethnidnatic spirit to the things he prepares. Give the same material to an Indian and a Siberian. Inevitably, each of them, with their own handwriting, will combine the ethnidnatic spirit within them with that material and turn it into something that fits the ethnidnatic spirit of their culture. Ethnidnatic spirits of things and objects are formed of this subtle difference.

A wooden handicraft related to Siberian ethnidnatism

A wooden handicraft related to Indian ethnidnatism

There are various ways to recreate the ethnidnatic spirit that is embedded in objects and materials. The first method will be to preserve the spirit of nature in that material. Accepting the shape, color, and image that we get from nature and the nature itself gives us will make our work easier. That pure and fresh energy in nature is so deep and inviolable that if a person tries to use it with malice and savagery, he immediately loses it. That's why, we must be very careful not to offend materials when we receive them from nature. The mass felling of trees and their use on the pretext of ethnidnatism are never in line with the teachings of ethnidnatism.

It is also possible to give the spirit of nature and life to incomplete and newly produced materials. For example, a piece of rock broken during production has lost the spirit of nature due to the interference of artificial materials (machine tools, etc.). It needs to be buried in the ground for recharging. Soil is a material through which life and death circulate. He gives life and energy to everything. You can see how the rock fragments that remain in the soil for a while accumulate energy. The duration can vary depending on the material and volume, but you can get the level you want by checking it yourself. Imagine the difference between two pieces of rock, one of which is left on the ground for a day and the other for a month.

If we want to use a piece of rock from nature for ethnidnatic purposes, we must also look at the environment surrounding it. The stone, which has long absorbed the energy of the environment, may not keep up with our ethnidnatic spirit. Therefore, after making a definite decision, the stone can be moved from its place. That stone, which is insignificant for us, can play a big role in terms of ecological and energy balance around it. Because we own that stone, we bring it to our house with love and use it just like we own a street animal ... If we throw it away from our house after a certain period of time, we must be ready for the karma of nature. People's insensitive and disrespectful attitude towards nature and their own ethnidnatic spirits has always led them to failure.

Every kind of material that has acquired the spirit of nature is suitable for representing any ethnidnatic spirit. The material without the spirit of nature cannot have the ethnidnatic spirit. Materials, objects, and things are just like human beings. Just as a person's ethnidnatic spirit is based on his ego, so the ethnidnatic spirits of materials are formed on the spirit of nature. The ethnidnatic spirit is, as we have always said, an image that can rest on the main spirit. Giving an ethnidnatic spirit to an object or thing that does not have a main spirit (the spirit of nature or ego) is just like dressing up a dead person.

The spirit of nature inside the material of object

Ethnidnatic spirit given to the object

Formation of the object with the spirit of nature with the ethnidnatic spirit

It takes at least 25 years for things and objects that do not have the spirit of nature to gain an ethnidnatic spirit. Even if these objects do not have the spirit of nature, they can have an ethnidnatic spirit by accumulating the energy given to them by the environment. In this way, obtaining the spirit of things and objects with an ethnidnatic spirit is considered a way of obsolescence. Plastic objects are usually regarded as objects that do not have an ethnidnatic spirit, however, such objects also accumulate the energy of the environment and people when they reach the age of 25 and form an ethnidnatic spirit.

ETHNIDNATISM IS NOT ONLY A PHILOSOPHY, BUT ALSO A STYLE

To regard ethnidnatism as philosophy or not is entirely up to the people who will be trained. It would not probably be the right approach to consider ethnidnatism as a philosophy as a whole. It is due to the fact that ethnidnatism regards all types of philosophy as way of thinking with an ethnidnatic spirit. It is formed of the unity of emotions and consciousness. The environment which forms consciousness gives it an ethnidnatic spirit, and emotions cause the emergence of ethnidnatic spirit. As a result, one loves the wisdom created by consciousness, positive emotions, and finally, by ethnidnatic spirit. The love of wisdom is called philosophy. That is why we shortly call ethnidnatism "philosophy." Whether ethnidnatism is accepted as a philosophy or not is up to humanity.

In the previous topics, we talked about how propaganda develops the ethnidnatic spirit. Propaganda is not only the propagation of ethnidnatism, but also the propagation of the ethnidnatic spirit within each individual, because the spirit belonging to each individual is different and marginal. This shows how colorful the mankind is. What is propaganda? Propaganda is the external reflection of the internal ethnidnatic spirit. You can show this reflection not only in the explanation, but also in various areas.

Different spheres are formed in style. Style is one of the main means of propaganda. Therefore, elements of art, architecture, music, and other styles can use the principles of ethnidnatism. The use of ethnidnatism must take place within the framework of its laws. Otherwise, it will be nothing more than a means of making money. Ethnidnatism, on the other hand, is responsible for preserving ethnidnatic spirits in all areas. This requires sensitivity in the areas where its name is used. Taking all this into account, we can conclude that this style can be applied in all areas, adhering to the principles of ethnidnatism. The areas in which ethnidnatism can be spread:

Ethnidnatic Fine Arts

- Ethnidnatic Architecture
- Other Types of Fine Arts

Ethnidnatic Types of Applied Arts

- Ethnidnatic Clothing and Jewelry
- Ethnidnatic Music and Choreography
- Ethnidnatic Literature
- Ethnidnatic Cinematography and Photography

Other Fields

- **Ethnidnatic Tourism**
- **Ethnidnatic Gastronomy**

Ethnidnatic Architecture (Spiritual Architecture)

One of the most influential factors to the environment, involved in the formation of ethnidnatic spirits, is architecture. The development of architecture varies depending on different geographies, periods, cultures, and climates. Every period, every culture, every geography, and every climate are the factors that contribute to the formation of the ethnidnatic spirit. This ethnidnatic spirit reflects the environment. The most obvious example of reflection is architecture. Architecture is periodically influenced by emerging ethnidnatic spirits and at the same time it affects these spirits. This, in turn, reveals the endless and constant circulation of architecture with ethnidnatism.

Ethnidnatism, which accepts every style of architecture as an ethnidnatic spirit, offers architectural solutions to those people who do not enjoy the same type of architectural style. These solutions can develop and satisfy their spiritual tastes. This is due to the fact that in modern times, all buildings are made in a similar style. However, in spiritual architecture, a common ethnidnatic spirit which more attracts the masses can be chosen. Of course, the constructions do not have to be the spiritual food of the whole society. It can be a group of people. What is important is the correct propagation of the chosen ethnidnatic spirit in the construction.

Almost all the buildings of the past 70 years have their own ethnidnatic spirit. This is due to the nostalgic feeling of the people who lived there. However, the main thing in ethnidnatic architecture is to be able to reflect this energy in the newly built buildings in accordance with the chosen style, along with functionalism. Unfortunately, there are thousands of architects who do not know the ethnidnatic rules but want to reflect this spirit. Therefore, ethnidnatism is a new periodic stage for architecture and architects. The buildings will be loved not only aesthetically, but also spiritually, with spiritual architecture. Large-scaled buildings which are similar to one another will no longer be able to radiate negative energy. Because there will be ethnidnatic architects who will feel their energy and influence on the spirits.

Example of Ethnidnatic Architecture: If you want to design a building in accordance with ethnidnatic principles, then you need to conduct a good research on the ethnidnatic spirit you choose. For example, the chosen spirit can be Sufi ethnidnatism. This current, which emerged after the establishment of Islam, is a very spiritual and complex one with ethnidnatic spirit. You need to understand what this current is based on. In Sufism, you have to learn about the lives and lifestyles of famous people. In this way, you can find out in what buildings and places they lived, which objects caused the rising of their ethnidnatic spirits.

The structure, material, and functionality of the building you are going to design in accordance with the Sufi concept will be fundamental principles in the design. The building should be attractive and make people who do not even know about Sufism feel the ethnidnatic spirit. The buildings, to be built in accordance with the principles of ethnidnatism, will nourish people spiritually, as well as provide lots of information about the ethnidnatic spirit to which they belong.

Writing a book on ethnidnatic interior and exterior architecture in detail is necessary for professionals who will be engaged in spiritual architecture. In this way, the projects of architects and designers will have not only functionalism, aesthetics, and style, but also the spirit they carry.

Other Types of Fine Arts

Ethnidnatic applied art can be found in many fields, but not every piece of art that attracts and is beautiful aesthetically, can be regarded as ethnidnatic art. Ethnidnatic art can exist, first of all, under the idea to which it refers. Art that does not originate from any ethnic, national, or ideological source cannot be considered ethnidnatic art. Today, people reflect their personal thoughts and lives through art, but ethnidnatic art must provide spiritual nourishment for general public, at least for a group of people. At the end of this process the spectator of the art object must be rewarded with an ethnidnatic uplift.

Ethnidnatic applied art is divided into different types based on the branches of art. This diversification is rather large, but it is possible to show some of its types:

- **Ethnidnatic Painting**
- **Ethnidnatic Sculpture**

Ethnidnatic painting can be applied by an artist-ethnidnatist who understands this philosophy. The principles of ethnidnatism must be combined with the creative, free aspects of the artist. The artist must pay attention to how his thoughts interact with his ethnidnatic spirit. Only after that he can accurately reflect his creativity and ethnidnatic spirit in the work. If his thoughts do not interact with the ethnidnatic spirit, he will not be able to create with necessary spirit. Creativity obtained only by thinking is an aesthetic image.

Ethnidnatic artists can work in different styles. In ethnidnatic painting the essence is not the style of work, but to which extent the work reflects the true ethnidnatic spirit to the audience. If the ethnidnatic spirit to be expressed is properly reflected in the work, that work cannot fail to gain value.

The works of many artists at different times survived and were appreciated and recognized for their unique ethnidnatic spirit. Nevertheless, the works that resembled the original and did not belong to any spirit were forgotten. In ethnidnatic painting, it is important to preserve the artist's marginality (ego) and the selected ethnidnatic spirit in a balanced way.

Although *ethnidnatic sculpture* has many similarities with painting, it has its own peculiarities. What are these features? Unlike artists, sculptors must be sensitive to the dynamics in order to keep their work in constant focus. If there is no dynamics in a work, then the ethnidnatic spirit in this work remains passive. An ethnidnatic spirit that remains in a passive state can achieve an ethnidnatic rising only if the statue is a statue with an ethnidnatic spirit known to all. However, in order to survive, it is important for statue to skillfully express the ethnidnatic spirit in dynamics.

Another distinctive feature of sculpture from painting is what the material used in the sculpture consists of. Material is also an important factor in painting, but in sculpture the material has a stronger effect. Each material has its own impact force. Sculptures made of metal, stone and marble have a strong influence on more monumental sculptures. Sculptures made of light materials such as wood, plaster and plastic are used in more decorative parts.

Simple statues erected to personalities, abstract statues and statues made only for aesthetic purposes cannot be attributed to ethnidnatism. If the statue has any ideological dynamics accepted by at least a group of people, then it is possible to attribute this work to ethnidnatism.

Ethnidnatic Clothing and Jewelry

The most ideal form of propaganda for ethnidnatic spirits is clothing. Clothing is a clear indicator of one's personality. Before we explain our personality and what ethnidnatic spirit we belong to, we express it in our clothes. It was the same before the beginning of the industrial era. People explained themselves adequately and properly with their clothes. The need to meet demands and the similarities brought about by production eliminated the need of propagation after a certain period of time. Although the clothes became functional, they no longer carried any spirit. Of course, experts in clothing and fashion want to create works that nurture ethnidnatic spirits, but this is not always the case for everyone.

Ethnidnatism takes a completely different approach to clothing. According to ethnidnatism it is important to make clothes in compliance with ethnidnatic spirits and to make the person who carries them alive in an ethnidnatic way. The ethnidnatic uplifts caused by clothing are superior to almost all the material objects we use in our daily lives. This is because clothes interact with body and spirit. Man feels happier if he wears clothes that belong to his ethnidnatic spirit, rather than the clothes which are fashionable.

The same clothing and trends in general fashion caused the need for ethnidnatism in people. Therefore, it lays the foundation for a functional, contemporary, spiritual fashion of ethnidnatic spirits. Clothes created in eth-nidnatic style are never out of fashion, on the contrary, they become more and more valuable. Because ethnid-natism requires original material, colors, and form of clothing.

Azerbaijan Ethnidnatic dress (by Rufat Ismayil)

The different form of clothing, made in accordance with the ethnidnatic spirit, their comfort and fit are important points. This is because uncomfortable clothing hinders the freedom and development of the soul, which in turn affects the ethnidnatic spirit. Clothing develops ethnidnatic spirit, and this development manifests its productivity in private life. Creativity, the quality of work of people with their ethnidnatic spirit benefit both the economy and the nature of the country in which they live. Loose clothes and adherence to the hanging principle are nuances that have a strong impact on ethnidnatic uplift.

Fibulas from Berber ethnidnatism

Unlike other fields of art, jewelry and jeweler's art have historically played a major role in shaping the ethnidnatic spirit of the people. For example, before primitive people made drawings on rocks, they used jewelry to form their own ethnidnatic spirits. Jewelry played a key role in shamanism, the primary belief of people around the world. Everything that hangs from the body carries an ideology, meaning and energy. As a human is an energetic being, he both represents and develops his own ethnidnatic spirit with every jewel used. Jewelry and gems always give an ethnidnatic spirit to a person. Therefore, kings and dignitaries used various jewels throughout history. The reason and secret of the use of jewelry was not only instruction and order, but also the highest level of the ethnidnatic spirit that belonged to them and the society they represented. If a person with status did not wear jewelry fitting the ethnidnatic spirit of his people, he would not be accepted by the society that he represented. In modern times, the concept of jewelry is just for instruction. Therefore, ethnidnatism considers jewels necessary not only for instruction, but also for the formation of ethnidnatic spirit. Although jewelry and original jewels (made of precious materials such as gold and silver, not bijouterie) may seem to depend on some kind of fashion, in fact, it is an independent form of art.

Ethnidnatic Music and Choreography

Music is considered to be the most useful field of art after clothing. Music takes the first place in ensuring the development of ethnidnatic spirits. Listening to ethnidnatic music has a positive effect on a person's creative activity. Music is believed to be the food of the soul, but it is the ethnidnatic spirit that transmits this food to the soul. If music does not correspond to the ethnidnatic spirit, then aggression, selfishness and other disorders appear in ego. Therefore, after exposing our subconscious self with ethnidnatism, we can find out what kind of music will benefit us.

The origins of music, its ups and downs, and its naturalness must be paid attention in ethnidnatic music. In modern times, there are different types of music and musical styles. Sometimes we think of the most suitable of these styles - the most prominent and popular. Therefore, we are far from natural music, the real food that nourishes the soul. But our ethnidnatic spirit, found in ethnidnatism, shows what kind of music nourishes us. We can be happier in this area, have a meaningful and qualitative life in which we can discover our abilities.

Natural music refers to music played with sound, filtered by a minimum of technological instruments. The sounds of musical instruments that keep the spirit of nature are natural sounds. Therefore, choose the most natural music for listening so that you can achieve spiritual development naturally. Since we are part of nature, we must pay attention to the naturalness of our food.

Performances should be nutritious, not harsh, and aggressive. Whenever one suddenly passes food to the stomach without chewing, of course, it makes a person sick. In some musical styles, we encounter harsh ups and downs. The ups and downs in music must provide an ethnidnatic rising.

Aggressive and depressive music has nothing to do with ethnidnatism and ethnidnatic spirit. Ethnidnatism is the art of being happy and making happy, which explains how important this cycle is for human beings.

In choreography, the inclusion of dance and show, along with music, raises the ethnidnatic energy to a higher level. That's why musicians make music videos to make music more understandable. In choreography the clothes must correspond to the ethnidnatic spirit, must be original and match the chosen music.

Ethnidnatic Literature

The fields of literature are wide, but what does ethnidnatic literature mean? Not all written works can be attributed to ethnidnatic literature. Ethnidnatic literature is considered to be purely spiritual literature. For example, if a poet or writer speaks about a region, a nation, and the ethnidnatic spirit that belongs to them, it can be considered ethnidnatic literature. In brief, examples of literature that do not express the ethnidnatic spirit, and the topic of which is an event, advice, or entertainment, cannot be attributed to ethnidnatic literature. If the example of literature is based on the expression of the ethnidnatic spirit about an event, it is considered ethnidnatic literature.

The fundamentals that express and represent the ethnidnatic spirit in the literature will be the words, terms, dialects, and descriptions of that spirit. If the descriptions and expressions are not used properly, then it will be considered a work with an incomplete ethnidnatic spirit.

Ethnidnatic Cinematography and Photography

We can feel ethnidnatic spirit in most popular, ethnic, national, and ideological films of the last twenty-five years. The direct ethnidnatic spirit of the directors really causes the audience to experience an ethnidnatic uplift. Directors should teach the world the subtleties of ethnidnatism. Ethnidnatism can confirm only the subtleties that directors pay attention to. Therefore, ethnidnatism has nothing to teach famous directors.

Photos and photography have become a pearl of modern art. This type of digital art, which reflects reality, also reflects ethnidnatic spirits. Taking photos at a time when the ethnidnatic spirit of places, people, creatures, landscapes, and many other things is maximized, makes the work spectacular and lively. Photos related to ethnidnatic photography are true reflection of the spirit of nature, any established ethnidnatic spirit in the photo. True reflection of the soul is sometimes not possible with a single photo. The transformation of the chosen ethnidnatic spirit into a form of gallery can propagate and define properly.

Ethnidnatic Tourism

Travels to different geographical areas have played a key role in the formation and development of people's ethnidnatic spirit. In the past, the purpose of these travels was only trade and occupation. In our time, when spirits are civilized and inclined to development, the concept of tourism has been formed. Tourism is a field that serves only to provide spiritual nourishment, as opposed to trade trips where only material needs are met. By traveling to other countries people are nourished by the ethnidnatic spirit of those places.

Tourism can be an excellent means in the search of an ethnidnatic spirit. People who cannot find their ethnidnatic spirit through research can achieve their goals through travel. The guardians and elements of ethnidnatic spirit are preserved in every geographical area. Getting acquainted with these elements and trying that lifestyle is an ethnidnatic journey.

Not all types of tourism can be regarded as ethnidnatism. For example, medical tourism, agrotourism, business tourism, and tourism related to night entertainment have nothing to do with ethnidnatism. Ethnidnatic tourism includes those types of tourism in which local food is available, such as visiting local people, visiting historical and important places as well as nature trips.

The main requirement for ethnidnatic tourism is that the places, objects, and items used in tourism, as well as the residents, should carry the ethnidnatic spirit related to that geography. The ethnidnatic spirit must be preserved in the design of hotels, in the conservation of places visited. Even a small custom, which is sometimes considered simple and insignificant to us, can be a great carrier of the ethnidnatic spirit.

Ethnidnatic Gastronomy

All the meals and tastes in the world have been associated with the development of ethnidnatic spirits. Nature played a significant role not only in a spiritual nourishment of people, but also in the satisfaction of their physical needs. Nature has provided human with shelter, clothing, and food. The climate of each geography determined the nature of the food, as well as the spirit of nature. The spirit of nature, formed by various regions, acquired an ethnidnatic spirit through their use by human beings.

People prepared food from nature according to their beliefs and tastes. Each preparation caused to form an ethnidnatic spirit in food. By passing down from generation to generation, prepared food, their types, and the rules of preparation included the ethnidnatic spirit brought by antiquity. Thus, gastronomy began to acquire an ethnidnatic spirit. The first supremacy of ethnidnatic spirit in gastronomy was observed in the palace kitchens.

In the palace kitchens, the best food corresponding to the most correct belief, was cooked in the most correct and delicious way. The cooks who prepared it added to each meal the noble spirit they had received from the palace. The preservation of the ethnidnatic spirit of the prepared food depended on the mood of the cook and the preparation of the food according to the ethnidnatic tradition. Today, some home-made local dishes are even tastier than those in the restaurants due to the preservation of the ethnidnatic spirit in them and the controlled transfer of energy to food. Adding love to food, in fact, has the same meaning as adding ethnidnatic spirit to food.

Sometimes we find out in history that the world's cuisines do not match at all. Normal dishes for some are considered abnormal for others. The positive or negative effects of historical processes have laid the foundation for the development, change and formation of the ethnidnatic spirit of cuisines.

For example, the troubles caused by wars in China, the growing oppression of the emperors led to the creation of a new cuisine among the people. Food that is not edible for many peoples of the world, gave rise to and formed a new Chinese cuisine with the courage they received from the ethnidnatic spirit of the Chinese. In the past, feeding on insects and reptiles, which was unusual for them, was considered a means of survival for a Chinese. Even eating the heart of a raw cobra, which is a manifestation of ancient beliefs, can be considered an ethnidnatic contribution of compulsion to the cuisine.

The unification of the ethnidnatic spirits of the peoples living in the Ottoman Empire and the transfer of the most beautiful culinary samples to the palace formed the Ottoman cuisine. In this cuisine it is possible to feel not only the cuisine of the peoples of Turkic origin, but also the ethnidnatic spirit of other people living within the Ottoman Empire with their food.

The most important rule in gastronomy is which ethnidnatic spirit the chef attributes the meal to and how sensitive he is to this meal. The composition and taste of food are different for each ethnidnatic group. Some ethnidnatic spirits promote their courage and strength with bitter and spicy food. There are also ethnidnatic spirits which express their courage and strength with dishes made with meat. Some kitchens, on the other hand, do not need courage, and give up adding meat and bitterness because they prefer spiritual development. In short, chefs and cooks with ethnidnatic practices in gastronomy can be more creative and proper with ethnidnatism in their work.

THE PRINCIPLE OF HANGERS IN ETHNIDNATIC STYLE

This principle plays a role of strengthening the ethnidnatic spirit in all areas with potential to be a style. The principle of hangers makes the ethnidnatic spirit more stable and stronger. This principle determines the sitting form of the soul. Ethnidnatic energy, strengthened by this principle, increases ethnidnatic sensitivity and accelerates uplift. What are the hangers?

Hanging objects from the existing object to the center of gravity of the Earth (downwards) are called hangers.

Hangers can be made of different materials due to each field. For example, materials that can be bent and hung like metal in architecture. In the field of clothing, we can take materials such as fabric, metal, leather. Hangers must be at least **1.2 times** longer than the objects on which they hang. In this way it is possible to create *an ethnidnatic aura*. The place where the hangers are attached must be strong, but it must be able to move under external influences. The dynamics created by the movement will activate the ethnidnatic aura and spirit. The wind or the movement of the object on which they are hung can move the hangers.

Example of whole hangers in history (from the sleeve)

The use of material hangers by Native Americans (from the sleeve)

Hangers can be whole or in fragments, depending on the object. For example, imagine a shirt, the sleeve of which can be hung 1.2 times looser than the shirt, it is considered a whole shape. The shirt can also fit the size of the sleeve, and we can create hangers in fragments by attaching extralong pieces to the sleeve. Hangers in fragments should be of noticeable size, much narrower than the length.

REPRESENTATION FUNDAMENTALS OF ETHNIDNATIC SPIRITS

Being human and having certain common characteristics as human beings are parts of the truth. As we accept this unity only physically, we do not pay much attention to the essence of the issue. As human beings, we are not just creatures with the same organs and emotions, there is another feature that unites us from the moment we exist. This feature is the existence of our ethnidnatic spirit. Thanks to the ethnidnatic spirit, we have different colors, different auras, different worldviews. We can declare this spirit, which saves the Earth from oppression and helps to develop our ego, to be the savior of our spiritual life.

The formation of ethnidnatic spirits in mankind can be attributed to the spread of people from Babylon to the world. Although many religious books, books of myths and legends deal with this legend, some facts prove that all people lived compactly in the past. The people who migrated to different areas, climates and geographies at different times were greeted by Mother Nature wherever they went. They also developed their ethnidnatic spirit in compliance with the place they lived. Those living in cold climate zones formed ethnidnatic spirits that required more active movement and physical strength, while those in hot climates formed more passive less physical force.

The differences between the ethnidnatic spirits formed in different regions made them sometimes enemies and sometimes friends. The reason for the hostility was a lack of empathy and proper expression. Although people tried to live in harmony with their ethnidnatic spirits, there was always hostility among them as they did not have the notion of ethnidnatism. Ethnidnatism has its own rules and principles that make everyone happy who understands and experiences it.

Pyramid of Representation

The rules and principles of ethnidnatism evolve with the release of the ethnidnatic spirits living within. Otherwise, evolution turns into a boomerang created by repetitions. We are living in this boomerang now. Many humanistic, multicultural measures have been taken to respect people's beliefs, cultures, nationalities, races, and ideas. Unfortunately, these measures, which are regarded only physical and mental by ethnidnatism, are not considered absolutely effective. The rules of humanism and multiculturalism taught to people are like the rules to be broken subconsciously. For example, in countries such as the United States, which has taken many measures against racism, racist thinking has not been completely prevented for decades. Racist thoughts are now and then calmed by anti-racist propaganda, but after a while they suddenly begin to reappear.

According to analysis of ethnidnatism it is concluded that restricting people with only mental, conscious, and logical propaganda is wrong. We are beings without restrictions, and we regard such simple anti-racist rules as boundaries. Therefore, the only effective way to free people from racist thinking is ethnidnatism. Because this current of spiritual thinking does not depend on any boundaries, absolute law, and insidious political expectations. Ethnidnatism is the coexistence of logic and spirit in one body.

The freedoms of ethnidnatic spirits are possible only on the basis of representation within human beings. Representation is an indicator of the freedom of a soul. A free spirit is called an ethnidnatic spirit if it represents itself without endangering others. The representation of spirit with hatred and anger within cannot be called ethnidnatism. The bases of representation of ethnidnatic spirits are as follows:

- *Silence*
- *Protection of aura*

- *Correct expression*
- *Love*
- *Respect*
- *Empathy*
- *Sharing*

The seven golden steps of the foundations of representation, each of which is as important as the seven chakras inside the human being, the seven heavens that never fall on mankind, are as important as the seven days of the week.

Silence is the beginning of creation, the platform of creation. Existence without silence is impossible, because it is possible to understand that something exists only in silence. The only difference between those who are oriented to the inner world and the ones oriented to the external world is that they can feel the silence with great pleasure. The most fundamental principle that ethnidnatism teaches people is to understand silence. Only a person who can be silent can learn how slowly the time goes and how to manage time. When we go fast in our chaotic life, it brings nothing but regret in the end. When we are governed by the principle of silence, we can understand how full and meaningful our lives are. There is an article in ancient Indian Sanskrit about "inactivity in activity, perception of activity in inactivity." In order to practice that Sanskrit, man only needs silence.

As the time flows, silence also reveals our ethnidnatic orientation. Sometimes we find ourselves with one or more ethnidnatic spirits we are inclined to. Based on the "self" we find, we can only think about how we can live in silence. Ethnidnatic representation plays a big role in our plans for living. Because ethnidnatic representation keeps our ethnidnatic spirit alive and does not allow it to die. Silence, one of the seven stages of ethnidnatic representation, is the basic layer of the representation pyramid. If the representation is based on chaotic state instead of silence, then under the influence of external factors ethnidnatic representation can quickly collapse. Ethnidnatic spirits with strong silence, can easily carry their representations. It is impossible for all mankind to learn the profundity of ethnidnatism in one day, that's why the representations of ethnidnatic spirits can be subjected to external interference.

No matter how difficult it is to restore silence, the result is as pleasant as the difficulty. Silence stands on the basis of all ideologies (religions, philosophical groups, beliefs, etc.), nations and ethnic groups. Their representatives- intellectuals, scientists, specialists, philosophers, saints are known only by their silence. Their essence has come out only in silence. This essence is like a large piece of diamond glistening at the bottom of turbid water. If there is silence, the water clarifies, and that shining diamond comes out. Ethnidnatism believes that there is such a hidden diamond inside every human being. It depends on human whether he constantly pollutes the water, or by clarifying it, reveals its essence. In this parable, the essence is our self-spirit and positive energy. Water is our ethnidnatic spirit. The clarification of water is a correct representation of the ethnidnatic spirit, and only then can it occur, only then can we reveal the essence. In other words, by finding their ethnidnatic spirit people can reveal the goodness within them.

Protection of the aura. People who have restored silence can step into the second stage of representation. Aura is the name given to the receptive and affective parts of the soul. Sometimes when we say we don't like someone's aura, we notice that person's energy has a negative effect on us. We can also call it the incompatibility of ethnidnatic spirits (aura incompatibility of ethnidnatic spirits) because human beings, who develop radicalism in their inner world, can have a negative aura. Their self-centeredness has given rise to a selfish ethnidnatic spirit. Free ethnidnatic spirits are more exposed to radical spirits when they use their receptive functions. At the end of the exposure, as we said, "Aura incompatibility of ethnidnatic spirits" occurs.

It is important to maintain a positive ethnidnatic aura and not to break the silence. The preservation of positive aura and silence in ethnidnatic representation creates conditions for the nourishment of ethnidnatic spirits. Arguments, egos, irritability, and the struggle against the negative effects of external factors are the greatest enemies of the ethnidnatic aura. Ethnidnatism believes that the fight against negativity is wrong. To put it briefly, we can express it as follows:

Do not stand against oppression, stand for peace. The power of peace will eliminate oppression anyway.
Aykhan AtaSak

The word that represents negative in the aphorism is "oppression". Those who stand against the negative are like those who block the flowing rivers. They live with the concern that the ever-growing river will one day destroy those who block it. Those who seek peace live in confidence and expect the triumph of their truth. This is what required in the ethnidnatic aura, to feel peace and to reflect it. If there is no peace in your ethnidnatic aura, then your ethnidnatic spirit will be inclined to deceit. Because negativity based on silence is the key to deceit.

Correct expression is one of the areas in which all humanity has a great trouble. Sometimes we see that many of the terrible and incomprehensible ideas and goals are not based on correct expression. We have even witnessed thousands of executions and crimes in history for the lack of correct expression. For example, looking at the life story of Joan of Arc, we can see how important the correct expression is for human life. However, Joan is considered a female heroine in France today and there is a magnificent monument erected to her.

The role of correct expression in ethnidnatical representation appears as a result of the subsequent regulation of silence and the aura. If people can express their ethnidnatic spirit correctly, then they can properly develop their ethnidnatic spirit. No matter how seemingly unnecessary the mental thinking of a society may be, it should not be considered the right approach to express the ethnidnatic spirit without knowing the opinions of the society. In order not to harm the ethnidnatic spirit within us, we must bring the expression as close as possible to the ethnidnatic spirit of the first society. After that, we can gradually express the representation that suits us best. This is called *the exposure process of ethnidnatic spirits*. As we have mentioned before, ethnidnatic spirits can be harmed by the incompatibility of auras. Correct expression and imposition will help to maintain a positive aura and silence.

There is a revivalist thought and spirit constantly hidden inside every human being. Ethnidnatism teaches people to release this mind and spirit, to live in harmony with their inner qualities. Because people are happy with their inner world. It is not enough for a person to have millions. However, living in harmony with the ethnidnatic spirit makes people happy and nourishes spirit. A person who achieves the correct expression is a person who takes the first step towards a happy life. Correct expression, which preserves a happy life and an inner ethnidnatic spirit, helps us not only in our spiritual life, but also in other spheres of our life. Any prestigious area we want, may not like "ourselves", but make sure that there are people in the world who share your thoughts. Ethnidnatism is aware that the development of the inner world plays a great role in the development of the material world. Because the motivation, positivity and orderliness of the inner world will affect the growth of working capacity, better learning, the development of creative spirit.

Love is the spiritual response we seek in everyone. The reason for the reciprocity is that love is a mirroring behavior. The types, areas, and expectations of love are different for each of us. One seeks love in a woman or a man, while love can be found in a small natural landscape for another. This is normal because individuals are different, because thoughts and inner spirituality are also different. There are times when we do not feel being loved in return to certain extent which we want, or we do not feel it at all.

The notion of love in ethnidnatism is different. Ethnidnatism, which can be formed within each individual, emphasizes that love can flourish not outside but in the inner world. Many events in life that hurt us, the progress that demotivates us, are caused by our expectations. Expectations are one of the wrong steps taken in human life. Removing expectations will make our life more comfortable and happier. It will also increase the good deeds we do without expecting anything in return. But the principle of "be good, do good", which stands on the basis of the creation of life, will manifest itself in your life, even if you do not want to. When life rewards you for what you do, it will give you a gift, even if you have no expectations. Your happiness is not fully guaranteed, because the existence of expectations reveals the psychology that life owes you.

This spiritual current also believes that the principle of "give love, see love" is wrong, because love given to all people does not result in the same reward. Sometimes, in return for love, we may be encountered with hypocrisy, ridicule, and rudeness. To live love within us is the best choice so that our expectations do not have a negative effect. Those who live within love will already treat others with love, so they will never be influenced by external factors. They will be able to easily preserve their ethnidnatic spirit. No matter what the ethnidnatic spirit you experience, remember that its essence is love. When love comes with silence, a positive aura, and the correct expression, respect, empathy, and sharing come with love. In the pyramid of representation bases of ethnidnatism, it is very important to understand this concept, which is a thin transition layer.

Respect. Love for the ethnidnatic spirits of others lays a foundation for respect. Ethnidnatic spirits are different, colorful, but sometimes they do not match at all. The discrepancy does not emphasize that ethnidnatic spirits should be enemies. The incompatibility of ethnidnatic spirits caused many wars in the world. Even people from the same nation and the same family opposed each other because of the incompatibility of ethnidnatic spirits. Respect in ethnidnatism does not mean only the respect for objects, ideologies, nations, ethnos, concepts, but also respect for that spirit, for that spirituality felt inside. The ethnidnatic spirit, which is the spirit of morality and spirituality, is the only salvation of mankind. People can attain supremacy only by enriching their inner spirituality.

Empathy is an opportunity to respect the ethnidnatic spirit and to make its existence longer. Empathy is the only means of further development of the spirituality. The cause of multiethnic spirits is empathy, the higher spirituality itself. Empathizing different ethnidnatic groups, experiencing them inside for a moment, enriches a person spiritually so much that he becomes a real intellectual.

Empathy is a habit-forming ability, a skill that everyone can acquire. It is a natural, instinctive ability like walking and speaking of a human being. Some of us have innate empathy, and some of us have acquired it from the family or at different stages of our lives. Unfortunately, there are people who have lost the ability of empathy or even do not have this ability. That is why wars are perpetrated and the persecution of human beings is considered normal. It is also gratifying that empathy is human-to-human. We can see this by looking at the development stages of the developed countries.

Although most Buddhist countries are materially undeveloped, we can see that spiritual concepts such as empathy and respect have existed for thousands of years there. To ensure the spread of empathy, it is enough to increase the ability to empathize the ethnidnatic spirits of others and to promote empathy. Basically, explaining to children what empathy is will help them to become an intelligent generation in the future.

Sharing is the final result of ethnidnatic propaganda. If you intend or share an object, a concept, a positive energy that belongs to your ethnidnatic spirit, then you are at the top of the representation pyramid of ethnidnatism. Sharing also paves the way for the compatibility of people. Throughout history peace agreements and reconciliation of countries and nations of many different ethnidnatic groups and their compatibility were realized by sharing something. Even today, politicians of different ethnidnatic backgrounds make great peace by sharing a small thing that promotes their ethnidnatic spirit. The sharing that keeps the world at peace is relevant and will be relevant at all times.

Aids and contributions to people, nature, culture and for the survival of ethnidnatic spirits are also considered sharing. Therefore, one can develop their ethnidnatic spirits with aids. Anyone who applies this pyramid step by step will see the benefits of the pyramid as long as he lives.

THE UNITY OF ETHNIDNATISM AND NATURE

The co-existence of living beings by conserving the form of creation is called Nature.

The notion of nature in ethnidnatism differs significantly in many areas. As ethnidnatism itself is a phenomenon, it also approaches nature from a phenomenal point of view. The concept of living beings and non-living things, which stands on the basis of the nature, is not explained in ethnidnatism in a way that everyone understands. We are taught that those that can move, grow, and feed are called living beings. We consider the opposite of all this to be lifeless. In short, trees, animals, plants, people are living, rocks, soil and water are non-living. In contrast to all this, there is not a concept of non-living things in ethnidnatism.

What does this concept refer to? The references are both their own principles and recent evidence of the vitality in various scientific fields. First of all, based on Physics, we see that the discovery of the atom has reflected the "principle of vitality of ethnidnatism" to this day. The movement of neutrons and protons around the nucleus of the atom is observed in all living and non-living objects. This proves the existence of an action. However, in previous teachings, we have suggested the existence of motion only as a feature of living beings.

The other fact is related with a great Japanese writer and researcher Masaru Emoto who revealed the secret of water to the world. Research proving that the molecular form of water is changed by human frequencies has once again proved to us that the objects and beings we consider inanimate are not inanimate.

It is observed that there is no concept of inanimateness on the basis of all ancient beliefs and widespread teachings. Even in Eastern beliefs such as Lamaism, Shamanism, Hinduism, Shintoism, and Taoism, we find out a more detailed explanation of the concept of vitality.

Ethnidnatism, like in Eastern beliefs, believes that objects are theoretically alive. There is only one difference. According to many Eastern beliefs objects in nature have only the spirit of ego. Ethnidnatism, on the other hand, claims that nature has its own spirit in natural objects. Because it is based on the phenomenon of nature having a common energy and spirit. The phenomenon of "Mother Nature", which is mentioned in all myths, is theoretically reflected in ethnidnatism.

The complex location of the elements of nature in one area provides the energy of this phenomenon. All objects, depending on a source, give rise to the concept of nature. Human has been closely following it since his creation. He has always had to remain faithful to the nature that has fed him for centuries and literally mastered him. Unfortunately, the increase in urbanization has made people forget this phenomenon. It is too late to realize that nature, which satisfies us physically, does not play only a physically nourishing role. Therefore, we have begun to build similar models of nature such as parks, gardens, and artificial plants in our cities.

The spirit of nature is the source of nourishment for all living beings, including a human. Nature, which we only regard a physical resource, is the source of energy for ethnidnatic spirits. Therefore, respect for nature will create the conditions for our identity and the opposite will lead us to become living dead souls. It is not correct to think that nature consists only of forests. Nature is any place where the human factor is not involved (desert, plain, submarine, etc.).

But can we feed on nature properly? 57% of the world's population live in cities. This indicator is growing every day. No matter how much artificial greenery grows, it does not fully reflect the spirit and complexity of nature. Therefore, people are malnourished. It also hinders the proper nourishment of ethnidnatic spirits. In short, although ethnidnatic spirits in cities are theoretically enriched, they do not develop in practice. The only way of feeding properly in cities is to conserve nature in the form of large areas near the city.

Another example is that the ethnidnatic spirits in the past were stronger than they are today. This is due to the wide scope of nature and how important people thought of nature in the past. Think of every member of humanity as a device, and nature is a great power plant, just as devices cannot work without electricity, so can people without the spirit of nature.

Sometimes people living in cities find it difficult to understand those living in villages. Urban residents think that the quality of life in rural areas is low, and people are not happy. However, the situation is the opposite, the villagers, who are more nourished by the spirit of nature than the townspeople, consider themselves happier. In cities, malnourished souls are more irritable because they are aggressive and selfish. Where there is nervousness and stress, there is no happiness. Life quality does not mean luxury cars, houses, etc., the quality of life is how happy you can be.

Not only the theory tells us that we are dependent on nature, but we also observe it with our instincts. Don't you think it's interesting that all men with hunting nature still go fishing, even though they can now buy everything in supermarkets? - Of course, it is not a coincidence, it is a gift of nature to our instincts.

Undoubtedly, not all the lifestyles of people in the world are far from ethnidnatism and its principles. The Japanese are the true example of the nation closest to ethnidnatistic thought. The lifestyle of the Japanese people, their devotion to nature and their own ethnidnatic spirit, can be an example of ethnidnatism for the world.

It is not difficult to observe the elements of the spirit of nature and ethnidnatic spirit in their beliefs. For example, the concept of the Zen spirit, attributed to Shinto thought, is a phenomenon that the spirit of nature tries to explain in ethnidnatism. In the concept of the Zen spirit, it is believed that there is silence and a positive spirit within any object that belongs to nature. In ethnidnatism the spirit of nature means the spirit of silence given by nature. The Japanese are a people who properly develop not only the spirit of nature, but also their own ethnidnatic spirits with proper rules.

It is necessary to use nature carefully in order to preserve its silence and inviolability. After all, we have accepted that all objects in nature are alive. When we use a piece of rock, we must not forget that it is alive. The use of only dead trees can prevent the mass felling of trees, which are the bulwarks of nature.

Ethnidnatism calls on humanity to respect sensitivity and identity. Because nature shows our identity. If we are not respectful and sensitive to nature, we can never have an identity.

THE STAGES OF SPIRITUAL PRACTICE

These stages show and explain the importance of spiritual practice in people's lives. Due to the different beliefs in the world, spiritual practice can be considered in two aspects: material and spiritual. Both aspects are able to give the same result in the end, as they depend on human faith. The power of faith always brings success.

From material point of view, spiritual practice can be viewed as a person's acquisition of positive habits through subconscious programming or inspiration. People are not mistaken from this point of view, because the human brain is the most magnificent computer that has ever existed. It is we who control this computer. When we learn computer programming, we can get everything we want. The human is capable of using even 100% of his brain in this way, and this seemingly unrealistic ratio again depends on our will and ability to do the right thing. You can also adopt spiritual practice itself as a kind of programming. Let's not forget that programming, as a result, is realized with the help of faith and direction of faith.

People approaching it from a spiritual point of view really believe in the power of the spirit and energy inside. The ethnidnatic spirit is perceived as an image of the ego. In ethnidnatism, spiritual practice plays a major role in the development of the ego, mind, and inner spirituality. Mastering the secrets of spiritual practice and knowing how to apply it is to achieve the seven levels of ethnidnatic representation more easily. High qualitative life again depends on us, our thoughts and how vast our inner world is.

Spiritual practice varies according to philosophies, beliefs, religions, and other systems related to this field. According to philosophies, the spiritual development is to allow the embodiment of right thinking. In many beliefs, it is to observe the boomerang of causes and results. Religions, on the other hand, view worship as a means for the development of spirit. In the world, each of the views from different perspectives has its own logical aspects, because internal energy can only develop through repetitive, observable practices.

Ethnidnatism, on the other hand, unites the concept of spiritual practice of all beliefs, philosophies, and religions in one point and views the issue more systematically. It explains the mystery of spiritual practice in the following order:

Perception - Idea - Thought - Belief - Feeling - Cognition – Living

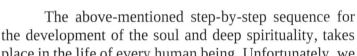

The above-mentioned step-by-step sequence for the development of the soul and deep spirituality, takes place in the life of every human being. Unfortunately, we do not often observe these processes when we know them, but observing simple concepts is tantamount to the awakening of mankind.

Perception is a process that occurs differently in all people and is also the primary reason why ethnidnatic spirits are of different colors. If everyone had understood the same idea in the same way, then we would not have differed from robots. Therefore, different perceptions are one of the factors that make a person human. In spite of the same source everybody grasps any book differently. Although books such as the New Testament, the Quran, and the Gita are one source, there are sects in the world that look at things from different angles. Even the worship, beliefs and rituals of these groups are different. Perception and comprehension are such big topics to talk about that it is possible to write a book about them in volumes. Therefore, we must observe our perception and perception of others. Increasing our perceptual abilities will lead us to a deeper spirituality.

Idea is an unanalyzed result of perception. The idea that passes through the filter of perception occupies the human mind in the form of that filter. Man's view of the world also forms his perception filter. The word "prejudice", derived from the Latin language (prior judgment), means that the perceptual filters are narrow. If a person has never read, his perception is limited. Various sources of information from the environment can substitute reading. The first time when thoughts and ideas come to mind, they are encountered with inner emotions. Perception of emotions forces the thought to be filtered again, and as a result the idea is forced to be thought again. When the thought is finished, it has either a complete or incomplete result. We can call it complete or incomplete thought.

Incomplete *thought* is caused by lack of information. Complete thought is the result of enough information that satisfies emotions. Discussions, facts, and affirmations are needed from time to time for the mind to develop and be fully made. Going through all the processes in its favor, thought gradually turns into belief. It is possible to change incomplete thought, but it is even more difficult to change complete thoughts.

There is a need for solid facts that enters the stage of *belief*, to change the way of thinking which often does not work. Belief is the last abode of the brain and logic. Belief is a form of consciousness. We cannot use our consciousness more than we believe. We cannot increase our faith beyond our consciousness.

Feelings and emotions are the energy phase of the body. The brain has already converted its physical activity into energy. The work of consciousness is based on the form of belief, it generates energy, and the body that feels it begins to recognize the inner spirit. He puts aside the idea that he is only made of flesh and bones. People who have not yet reached the emotional stage are more likely to do logical analysis than those who are in the emotional stage. Because the mind needs to rely on belief, which is a form of functioning. Meeting the needs leads to a safer and more complete sense of accomplishment. Mastering emotional control is the first step towards spiritual practice. Using only emotions should be considered a wrong step. This is because using the energy of the senses in spiritual practice without directing it can lead to the wrong development of the soul.

Cognition is the co-mechanism of emotions, beliefs, and logic. Cognition is a model of perceiving an idea not only by belief and logic, but also by feeling. People who reached the level of cognition belong to the class of intellectuals. The proper development of the soul and the ethnidnatic spirit is possible only through cognition. People who have reached the level of cognition are more able to observe their ethnidnatic and egoistic spirits than at other stages. They can give a more correct direction to its development.

Living is considered a higher level of cognition, and cognition is considered wiser by constant practice. A person is considered to be the highest ethnidnatist if he lives his life being aware of his own ethnidnatic spirit. The long-term understanding of ethnidnatic spirits is the best example of ethnidnatic spiritual practice.

All the exercises recommended for spiritual practice (worship, meditation, philosophy, etc.) go through these processes. Only those who know these processes and want to develop their spiritual practice both ethnidnatically and personally should be aware of these stages. Brains observing this can determine the course of the process in all directions. Knowing at what stage you are will make it easier for you to develop your inner world.

ETHNIDNATIC SPIRITUAL PRACTICE

In order to understand this topic, we must activate our brain with a series of questions. We can get the essence by activating the brain which is the most active part of the soul. Only the questions which cause uplift can increase the thinking ability of brain.

"Are you aware of your existence in life?" "What does existence mean for you?" "I am a human and what are my aims as a human?" "What are the reasons for my being human?" "Why was I born in this period?" Choose one of these questions, put the book aside and think about it for a moment...

Such kind of activating questions are so effective that they cause awakening immediately. Because the spirit increases its molecular existence in the awakened brain. After that human begins to perceive everything not with material consciousness but with spiritual consciousness. Have you ever been able to find answers to these similar questions mentioned above? Of course, if you ask 8 billion people in the world the same question, you can get 8 billion different answers with some common features. The question is not in which aspect the answer is correct. Here the question is how useful the answer is for us. Ethnidnatism responds it in the following way:
Breathing, moving, speaking, thinking, and reacting are not enough for a human being to realize his existence. It is due to the fact that material consciousness which controls them always functions how to perform technical work more properly. It is spiritual consciousness which inspires us, which is the source of our emotions, which stands on the basis of our creative activity and the most important, which teaches us our "Ego". Only spiritual

consciousness can distinguish us from others. Our features can be determined by the flow of the spirit inside us.

Materialization of human, the failure of life and his adaptation to daily chaos result in regret in the end. Sometimes it is too late to ask a question: "Why have we lived the whole life?" Living the life for one purpose and choosing the ideal mission for us result in living the life more meaningfully. There are people who live all their lives for earning money, in the end they regret that they have lived an incomplete life. These people, who feel incomplete, need to be completed. Those who do not serve their souls even once in their lives generally feel that there is no happiness. As a result, they seek happiness in materialistic areas.

The factor of being human is not only physical feature. There is also a person's morality and ethnidnatic spirit, which ensure human's happiness. Of course, ethnidnatism, based on the words of some self-proclaimed "philosophers," does not consider it right to turn away from means such as money that have a positive effect on people's living standards. Because it is necessary to have certain physical standards in order to ensure the formation of the spirit. You have to work to ensure that standards are met. But love your work. If you are working on something that hurts you spiritually, leave it. Your favorite job will not tire you out and you will have enough time for spiritual practice.

In brief, plan your life not only to meet your physical and material needs, but also to meet your spiritual needs. If possible, try to change the environments that do not suit your ethnidnatic spirit. If the scale of the place you are going to change is large, first try to change it with people in the same ethnidnatic spirit as you, without anyone's objection. If you can't do that, or you can't find people who share your ethnidnatic spirit, then leave that environment. Living in an environment that suits your ethnidnatic spirit is a precondition for you.

The development of ethnidnatic spirits in the right environment will prolong the number and duration of its ethnidnatic uplift. People who practice ethnidnatic uplift a lot become energetically and spiritually strong. People with strong morals increase willpower, endurance, silence, happiness, and sensitivity. Strengthening the will is to give up bad habits and gain good habits. Therefore, an environment conducive to the ethnidnatic spirit and with a large number of ethnidnatic uplifts are necessary for a quality of human life.

Another issue in ethnidnatic spiritual practice is finding the right ethnidnatic spirit. By finding the right ethnidnatic spirit, you can make spiritual practice more productive. It sometimes takes a long time to make sure that the right ethnidnatic spirit is found, but each of us knows about our tendencies approximately. The first tip for us is to know what kind of music, clothes, philosophy, and ideas we like.

The processes for the development of the accepted ethnidnatic spirit are as follows:

- *Looking around with the eyes of existence;*
- *Ethnidnatic meditation;*
- *Ethnidnatic activities;*
- *Visits and trips.*

Looking around with the eyes of existence. How well do we know ourselves? Are we just the reflection we see in the mirror? Or is the person we portray inside us different?

Do not look for the answers to the questions far away, because the answer to the questions you ask is still inside you, in your existence. The moment when a person begins to live a free life is, in fact, the moment when he realizes himself. Otherwise, man never has what he calls life and longevity, he just wanders around. Here is the secret of a quality of life, and here you understand what you want to achieve. Giving priority to education in expensive colleges, luxury cars, villas, a beautiful career always makes us confused. In the environment in which we were born, we were taught that only the adornment of the material world is life and us.

Tell your children to find out first who they are in order to start living, or they will need you for the rest of their lives. Very few parents realize that only children who find themselves achieve what they want. Look at your children not as "it's just a child," but as a carrier of a precious spirit within. Only then can your child easily find out who he is. Ethnidnatism always emphasizes the freedom and value of the spirits within. This is because the body will one day disappear, but the spirit, which is the energy that moves the bodies, will never disappear.

People who find their "selves" enjoy even the smallest values of life. However, in our time, everything that people enjoy depends on size and quantity. Only in this way we have to measure happiness. According to ethnidnatism, taste depends on the inner world, not the outer world. People who have a wide and independent inner world can enjoy even the smallest processes of the outer world with great effects.

You need clear eyes to see what the taste is. Feel the energy inside you, assuming you are in a box. The environment outside the box is called life. You try to look out of the box. At this point, you will see that you are superior and free, rather than being a physical being. This is the moment, the moment of existence. The view from the inside to the outside world is called "looking around with the eyes of existence."

The benefit of "looking around with the eyes of existence" to ethnidnatic spirits is to ensure that the ethnidnatic spirit, which regards ego as a ground for itself, can stand on a more absolute ground. Looking with the eyes of existence is the door key to the spiritual world. Those who do not have a key cannot enter through this door.

Ethnidnatic meditation. Everyone who passes through the door of existence finds himself in the meditative world. The ethnidnatic spirit helps to understand existence. Ethnidnatic spirits play a great role in the meditative world.

Meditation is the moment when the free spirit unites with the higher consciousness. Most people in the world think that meditation belongs only to Indians and Tibetans. It is true that Indians and Tibetans are far ahead in meditation, but it is possible to find meditation in all cultures and philosophies. Meditation is not just a matter of closing eyes and concentrating on something. Meditation is a means for the spirit of ego to reach the highest level.

As we mentioned before, many people think that meditation belongs only to Indians and Tibetans. This misconception prevents souls from reaching a higher level through many meditations. Therefore, ethnidnatism recognizes that this concept is completely wrong, that every culture and philosophy have its own style of meditation. Styles change according to the forms of ethnidnatic spirits.

Meditation on the colors of ethnidnatic spirits is ethnidnatic meditation. Ethnidnatic meditation is the use of the accepted spirit in meditation, which is different from usual Indian and Tibetan meditation. The use of the spirit is known only to those who have deeply experienced that ethnidnatic spirit.

Auxiliary means of ethnidnatic meditation can be melancholic music, places and nature belonging to that ethnidnatic aura, which create ethnidnatic uplift in ethnidnatic spirits. One of the main rules of ethnidnatic meditation is the compliance of the position with the ethnidnic spirit. Anyone can easily take the "lotus" position, which corresponds to all ethnidnatic spirits.

There is ethnidnatic meditation in every ethnidna

Active and passive mudras can also be used in meditation. Mudras help to regulate the flow of energy in the body, and we can use the appropriate mudras. Another point recommended in ethnidnatic meditation is that in the use of mudras, our ethnidnatic spirit determines the mudras for us according to the direction of its flow. Many yogis and spiritual practitioners recommend gap meditation. However, gap meditation is nothing more than a walk in the inner world. For this reason, it is right to meditate at a certain point. There is a point in the practice of meditation that Ayhan AtaSak would recommend to all ethnidnatists, and this point can be considered more correct. He expresses this point in his aphorism: *"Meditation is the worship to the power in the depths of life in the mind."*

Finding strength in the depths of life and drawing strength from it according to one's own ethnidnatic spirit is considered to be the highest level of spiritual practice. All philosophies, religions, and teachings explain the infinite power of the universe and the depths of life in their own way. Ethnidnatists can get the energy they need to develop their ethnidnatic spirits from the depths of life through meditation. This will speed them up to a higher level.

Those who have reached a high level of ethnidnatic spirit are considered high-ethnidnatists. Their lives are deeper and more productive. Productivity enhances creativity, and a shared product gives pleasure to a person who shares it and to the one with whom it is shared.

Ethnidnatic activities are considered to be activities that affect the development of our ethnidnatic spirits in our daily lives but were abandoned due to modern requirements. We can show blacksmithing as an example. Blacksmiths used to perform their work in accordance with the people's spirits and daily needs. The order of each man along with the desire and spirit within him, with labor and the energy of the creative master formed the iron. The ordered goods supported the user morally because he ordered it in his own spirit.

Hand-made objects created by us on a household basis is more valuable to us than those that come out of automatic machines. This is because we share our ethnidnatic spirits in what we make. Objects that are automated and can meet only physical requirements are soulless. Therefore, it can never meet our spiritual needs.

There is a wide range of activities, and the main thing is to be able to determine which ethnidnatic group the activities correspond to. Riding a horse, preparing something, or cooking can be considered an ethnidnatic activity, but if it does not conform to the established ethnidnatic spirit, it cannot be considered an ethnidnatic activity.

Pilgrimages and visits have been considered for centuries as a means of developing ethnidnatic spirit, being unaware of it. Mandatory visits are not for the development of ethnidnatic spirits, only voluntary visits can be considered as such.

The secret here is that the energy flow accumulated at the place of pilgrimage nourishes people. Nature always feeds people everywhere, but there are some places that people have created and chosen for themselves, and visiting these places both develops and nourishes people. Throughout history, people have created various monuments and landmarks in these places. Monuments and signs were used to make it easier to locate and identify energy sources.

Voluntary visits and pilgrimages nourish ethnidnatic spirits and they have a great impact on the development of spirits. The so-called ethnidnatic spirit - the spiritual energy accompanies us wherever we go. The development of our spirit only depends on it. During travels, individually or in groups, a person interacts with the place where he goes, as if they exchange something. As a result of this spiritual exchange, both the energetic place and the spirit that feeds from it get satisfied, because they strengthen each other.

Even before ethnidnatism, ethnidnatic spirits tried to do something for their own development. However, the emergence of ethnidnatism, the knowledge that people have their own ethnidnatic spirits, will accelerate this development. Man will develop not only physically but also spiritually.

THE USE OF ETHNIDNATIC SPIRITS FOR NEGATIVE PURPOSES

The ethnidnatic spirits formed by mankind are like a big tree. The concept of man is like the core of the tree, and belonging to any ethnidnatic spirit is a branch of it. Each main branch creates conditions for the smaller branches to live together, and the other branches repeat the same for other smaller branches that depend on them. The world hierarchy also works in such a system. In short, geographies, the peoples who live in them, small ethnic groups within nations, and other people with different ethnidnatic groups in large societies - we are all branches of the same tree as human beings.

Diversification of ethnidnatic spirits like branches of a tree, their differences, no matter how different and private they were, made them enemies of each other with the courage caused by ignorance. Therefore, people easily murdered each other simply because they did not understand each other's ethnidnatic spirit. At times, these murders turned into major genocides and crimes. The killing of people belonging to one ethnidnatic spirit, simply because they experience their own ethnidnatic spirits, is a fundamental principle of human injustice. Millions of people around the world still suffer from this principle.

In history, the most dangerous process for people hating one another because of their different ethnidnatical spirits has been to use ethnidnatic spirits for negative purposes. Many revolutions in history broke out with the help of ethnidnatic spirits. Of course, there were positive sides of these revolutions. People subjected to oppression had the right to make revolutions, and it was their ethnidnatic spirits that inspired these revolutions and brought people to the squares. The ethnidnatic uplift of these spirits overcame the fear within them and made them stronger.

The people who defended their lands and rebelled because of being persecuted are exceptions. Some ethnidnatic groups oppressed humanity by claiming to be superior. This negative ethnidnatic concept, which caused many murders in the world, has always dragged humanity into the abyss. Ethnidnatism explains what negative ethnidnatism is so that humanity will no longer be under the oppression.

Let us take historical examples of the use of pure ethnidnatic spirits for negative purposes. The greatest example of the use of ethnidnatic spirits for negative purposes in history is Hitler's Nazi ideology. Hitler misused the ethnidnatic spirit of his people to turn them into participants in great crimes. Although he was unaware of the philosophy of ethnidnatism, he turned his ethnidnatic spirit and ideology into philosophy. He formed principles based on his ethnidnatic spirit and presented these principles to his people as the ethnidnatic spirit of the "Superior Aryan Race". Some people, who did not understand the essence of the ethnidnatic spirit, declared him "Ruler". He used the ethnidnatic spirit of the people to force them to commit terrible crimes. When it became clear that his real goal was nothing but to commit crime and selfishness, it was too late.

Hitler and Northern ethnidnatism to which
he encouraged his people

Negative ethnidnatism became the biggest weapon of dictators such as Hitler. Is there any relation between true German ethnidnatism and Hitler? Certainly not. After the victory of the German people over their dictatorship, their true ethnidnatic spirit is correctly expressed in modern time. Today, the country where millions of people from around the world have found refuge is an example of true German ethnidnatism. Because ethnidnatism is based on principles such as kindness and sharing.

Some Armenian representatives, who turn their ethnidnatic spirit into an organization, are also true example of it. This group, which always thinks that Armenian ethnidnatism is superior to other examples of ethnidnatism, always uses the ethnidnatic spirit of the Armenian people to attack other nations. One of the biggest examples of this attack is the Khojaly genocide, the Holocaust of the Caucasus, in which babies were removed from the wombs of pregnant women, and infants were raped and killed. Of course, we cannot blame all the Armenian people. There are supporters of peace in every nation. But anyone who wants to use the Armenian ethnidnatic spirit for negative purposes and revives Nazi ideology is guilty. It is a Nazi ideology that teaches the Azerbaijani and Turkish enmity to the children with a great hatred at an early age. This hostility resulted with more than 1 million people fleeing their homes and they have become refugees and internally displaced people nowadays.

Khojaly genocide

Ethnidnatism warns humanity not to misuse the purity of ethnidnatic spirits. The unjust death of one person means the death of all mankind. Therefore, if you feel hatred and you do not want the result to lead to the unjust death of a person, cleanse it from your ethnidnatic spirit. The most ideal tool for cleansing is empathy meditation. Empathy meditations, or a simple moment of empathy, will cleanse your ethnidnatic spirit off hatred. Purified ethnidnatic spirits will never be complicit in crime.

THE SYMBOL OF ETHNIDNATISM

"Symbols are the keys to the doors of energy."
The founder of ethnidnatism Aykhan AtaSak

There have always been symbols since the existence of mankind. There are several symbols that can be found all over the world. When we look at the early history of mankind, we see that today symbols are given less importance. It used to be even so important that people sacrificed themselves for the symbols and ideologies formed by symbols.

What have symbols brought to mankind? Symbols sometimes bring unity, sometimes mercy, sometimes information, sometimes oppression. What is real is the direction in which the symbols are used. A symbol can be used for bad or good purposes. How powerful the use is, and the activation of the symbols depends on the person. For some, symbols are seen as an expression, for others as a spiritual support, and for others as a source of energy. It is not important what the symbols are used for, but for what purpose they are used.

At first, symbols were used for religious, mystical and ethnidnatic purposes. People used symbols either to strengthen the worship of their gods, or to achieve some mystical goal, or reinforce their ethnidnatic spirit.

If we look back at the history, we observe that the use of symbols for mystical purposes has lost much of its influence. Symbols are used only as a means of information and expression for religious purposes. However, there is no change in the use of symbols for ethnidnatic purposes. Each ethnidnatic current defines its own symbol, develops it, and as a society unites around that symbol. Uniting around a symbol, it imposes a certain energy on the characters, structure, and form. Of course, energy loading does not happen in a short time. This will take some time and effort. Symbols belonging to one person have a very weak effect.

Symbols of ethnidnatic spirits and currents are only useful for the development of people with an ethnidnatic spirit. It is impossible to influence the development of others. If it is used for negative purposes within an ethnidnatic current and a negative load is placed on the symbol of that current, then this symbol may have a negative effect on people belonging to that current. Even after a certain period, it can bring misfortune to those people as karma.

Ethnidnatism explains some details of symbols in order to carefully select and analyze the symbols to be used in all new currents. This is because people who activate it using symbols should not spread negative energy around and unknowingly disturb the ethnidnatic balance of others. All people use symbols mostly to represent and develop their ethnidnatic spirits. This is related with easy balance of the represented spirit with symbols. A balanced ethnidnatic spirit, on the other hand, empowers the spirit of ego.

There are also some symbols that are used only to convey information. The symbols and logos of companies and enterprises are examples to them. These symbols have no energetic effect. They are only stored in subconscious mind for a long time.

As symbol of ethnidnatism has simple structure and features, it might have been previously used in certain currents. The question is not how it was perceived in the past, but how ethnidnatism defines this symbol. We can briefly explain this definition as follows:

"Mankind and its bulwark of spiritual perfection are the foundation of peace and unity."

Although this definition describes the symbol of ethnidnatism briefly, let us explain it to our readers in more detail: in the analysis of symbols, it is necessary to explain the parts separately according to the numerological sequence, or it is impossible to fully understand the symbol. The symbol of ethnidnatism, as its name suggests, consists of three parts.

The first is the column of spiritual perfection at the center. The perfection of man, his belonging to spirituality, which is the energetic form of perfection, made him superior. A superior person is a person with morality and perfection. If perfection and spirituality do not develop within him, he is considered an incomplete superior person. The superior man is always free and independent. To do this, we symbolize him and spiritual perfection as a single column.

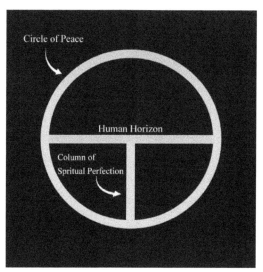

The meaning of the Symbol of Ethnidnatism

The horizontal part symbolizes the sky, uniting mankind, and spiritual perfections. The column of spiritual perfection and the "T" shape of the sky maintain the balance of the earth. If there are no superior people and spiritual perfection in the world, the sky will collapse, and the balance of the earth will be disturbed. You can also see the whole humanity in "T".

The circle represents peace, unity, and the universe. Both our spiritual perfection and the whole world are a part of this universe. The circle is also used to reinforce all the characters. Circle orientation makes it more comfortable and faster. Ethnidnatism has used the circle to increase people's inclination to supremacy.

Wishing to live in a world where there are more superior men, and spirituality is balanced with perfection.

HUMAN ETHNIDNATISM

What is human?! Have you ever asked this question? Why were free spirits imprisoned in bodies with restriction? It is as if this ancient world was a colorful, big prison in our subconscious. Sometimes we do not find freedom anywhere. Even a view of the horizonless plains does not satisfy the love of eternity in our eyes. We look for freedom, silence, and eternity everywhere. Therefore, we connect the end of all philosophies and religions, even that unknown death, with eternity. What if we are looking for eternity in the wrong place? Has it ever been asked? Every superior brain that understands eternity knows that eternity begins with awakening. Death is not the end, but a simple change for them. The destruction and termination of objects have always caused meaningless fear. This senseless fear is in fact the fear of an eternal soul that has no purpose in life and has not been able to reveal its essence. The spirit does not live with the fear of change, but not being able to accomplish his highest goal in time.

The immaterialized soul, which has been in search since childhood, is always subconsciously searching for eternity and purpose. Materialization and adaptation to the world have always been a barrier to the goal.

Those who have found their missions and live up with their ethnidnatic spirits freely are immortal. How happy they are! Horizonless plains and endless seas are eternal for them. This eternal energy, which harmonizes the inner eternity with the body, has nothing to fear, because it has found eternity within. He no longer finds paradise in other places, but in and around himself.

The souls who remember their missions and instinctively have kept them since childhood are pure. They are the pillars of the earth, the guardians of goodness. They are never ashamed to experience their ethnidnatic spirits or mix it with negativity. Everyone is nourished by the energy they radiate and unites all ethnidnatic groups on one platform. This platform is "human ethnidnatism."

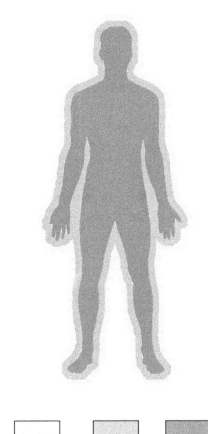

| Ethnidnatic Spirit | Human Ethnidna | The spirit of ego |

Levels of spirit and human ethnidna

Human ethnidnatism is both a physical and a spiritual interpretation of being human, being a person. Just as the nature is the mother of all ethnidnatic groups, so the father is human ethnidnatism. This is because the diversity of nature influenced human ethnidnatism and gave birth to other ethnidnatic spirits. Ever since we realized that we are inhabitants of the earth, we have realized that we are human and that we experience humanity as a soul.

We have always given the theorem of ego to the ethnidnic spirit. It is true that the ethnidnatic spirit is the image of ego, but even in ordinary life, we know that the most delicate image consists of several levels. Human ethnidnatism can be considered the lower level of this image. Because how can we experience our ethnidnatic spirit properly if we do not realize that we are human and different from other creatures?

The ethnidnatic soul that does not experience human ethnidnatism is just as harmful to the ego as an outfit without a lining to the body. When we analyze souls which are ethnidnatic but have forgotten humanity, we can see how careless, cruel, and racist they are. People are not able to freely express their ethnidnatic spirit because of them, as no one wants to look racist and cruel.

Human ethnidnatism explains its features to make people realize that humanity is not only a physical and emotional factor, but also a spiritual factor. Man is distinguished from other beings not only by his consciousness, but also by the fact that he belongs to a special spirit. This distinguishing feature is the highest quality of a person.

While analyzing people, one can find out many features of human ethnidnatism. These features distinguish it from other living things. For example, a person's desire to walk. No living being walks in an unknown direction, if it is not needed, but human walks. When a person walks and thinks while walking, he subconsciously or consciously remembers that he is a human being. This memory gives him a special pleasure. Therefore, everyone prefers to walk, regardless of direction or location.

Walking in the lap of nature brings us closer to human ethnidnatism. The combination of nature and human ethnidnatism radiates great energy as a unity created by male and female energies. Therefore, we can find human ethnidnatism only when it meets nature. It is impossible for human ethnidnatism to exist without nature. In our time, the unnatural nature of urbanization has led to the weakening of human ethnidnatism. Human ethnidnatism, which belongs to the male energy, needs the nature which is the female energy itself. When its demands are not met, it becomes weak. Therefore, people living far from nature, only in an urban environment, are cold-blooded towards other people.

We mentioned that the people who experience human ethnidnatism more are those who live in villages and in the lap of nature. Therefore, when we go to a village, we can see how people with less wealth are happier and warmer. These people, united with nature, are not only warm-hearted, but also hospitable and caring, because they experience human ethnidnatism deeply. They are the first to remember that you are a human being, regardless of your nationality or ethnicity. Are the people in the city like that? No, because they experience human ethnidnatism less, they only criticize each other's ethnidnatic spirits and carry out their analysis by appearances.

Ethnidnatism explains the role of nature in human life in order to increase people's responsibility for nature.

Let man without nature realize that he is lonely, without a mother.

Superior ethnidnatists are the guardians of human ethnidnatism. Their task is to explain to people the depth of human ethnidnatism and to propagate human ethnidnatism everywhere. Therefore, superior ethnidnatists with their long hair, adhere to the principle of hangers-on, representing how they are connected to nature everywhere. Their braids represent mother tree, a symbol of nature and the universe, from heaven to earth.

Loose clothes that they wear always make them aware of their inner spirits. They always remember that they are human beings and superior spirit. Was it the same in ancient times? People who adjusted their lives to their thoughts and freedom also reflected it in their appearance, because they did not have smartphones or televisions to watch. Instead, they had brains to think.

You can find superior ethnidnatists meditating in a corner of nature which can seem meaningless to you. This is because they are the reminders of nature which is forgotten. In doing so, they increase the balance between humanity and nature in the Earth.

They have special eyesight, the ability to see the unknown with the naked eye. They will immediately notice what you cannot see. They are always looking for happiness not in the outside world, but in the inner world, and they are happier than many, even in their worst days. A lonely rock or tree in the farthest corner whispers to them so they can hear and start talking.

They are friends of nature, all flora and fauna. The feeling that they are responsible for protecting them is always innate. It is possible to find these qualities in superior ethnidnatists and in every person who is on the way to become a superior ethnidnatist.

TERMS AND CONCEPTS USED
IN ETHNIDNATISM

In ethnidnatism **ethnidnatic spirit** is accepted as the highest level of human spirit. It is an exception that creates national, ethnic, and ideological emotions of people. Thanks to the ethnidnic spirit, the human self is nourished energetically, thus avoiding aggression, ego, and tension. You can also see the ethnidnatic spirit as a nourishing image of the ego. Ethnidnatic spirits vary according to each nation, geography, ideology, and even the individual.

Experiencing the spirit in an ethnidnatic way is the process of letting the ethnidnatic spirit, which is not possessed, live for a moment or for a while. Empathy is the highest state of mind and ability.

The mirror theorem is the process of representing the possessed spirit in accordance with the subtleties of that ethnidnatic spirit. According to the mirror theorem, the ethnidnatic spirit inside a person is reflected by a human like a mirror to the outside, and he even enriches it by making additions to the ethnidnatic spirit.

The ethnidnatic spirit created by the environment can also be called the "innate ethnidnatic spirit". It is the first ethnidnatic spirit that people possess, depending on their birthplace. Environmental factors and environment play a key role here.

The journey of the ethnidnatic spirit occurs when people are inclined to ethnidnatic spirit that is different from the spirit created by the environment. Basically, he seeks to relive the ethnidnatic representations he has never seen before, as if he had lived them before. As a result, a person who travels for a moment acquires a foreign ethnidnatic spirit that he is inclined to.

Ethnidnatic deficiency syndrome is caused by inability to fully regulate the inner world and the malnutrition of the ego. Man's inability to find out who he is and what kind of ethnidnatic spirit he possesses results in the malnutrition of the ego. The symptoms of this syndrome in total are often attributed to various and separate psychological diseases. In fact, the symptoms directly indicate the presence of this syndrome. The symptoms of the syndrome include internal anxiety, tension, stress, emotional detachment, a feeling of exhaustion. The syndrome arises from a chaotic lifestyle and not feeding the spirit of ego through the ethnidnic spirit. The only solution is to nurture the spirit of self and search for the ethnidnatic spirit.

Ethnidnatic uplift is a high feeling of belonging to certain object and event when we come across this event or object. The feeling of belonging leads to euphoria, emotional confusion, and upward movement of energy flow from the body. All these are signs of ethnidnatic uplift. A person who enjoys the moment of uplift spiritually wants to live that moment more. It is because his ethnidnatic spirit has sufficiently nourished the spirit of self. Ethnidnatic uplift leads to the increase of creativity and new inspirations.

Freedoms are said not to interfere with the representation of ethnidnatic spirits, to live up with any ethnidnatic spirit as much as they want. Thanks to freedoms, people live in accordance with their ethnidnatic spirit, and they are neither influenced by external factors nor pay attention to the influences.

Restrictions are said to prevent the representation of ethnidnatic spirits by external factors and to pay attention to the effects of external factors. Due to the mentality of the society in which they live, people cannot live up with their ethnidnatic spirit freely.

The search for an ethnidnatic spirit is a process for those who are unaware of their ethnidnatic spirits or who have not found their ethnidnatic spirits correctly. In this process people look for their ethnidnatic spirit in appearance, philosophy and in the style of music they listen to. People who find their ethnidnatic spirits can continue to search for other experiences and spiritual riches throughout their lives.

The artificial ethnidnatic spirit, in short, means "imitation." Imitating the ethnidnatic spirit of others, trying to live it by force, even if it is not inherent in its nature, creates an artificial ethnidnatic spirit.

When a person possesses only one ethnidnatic spirit, it is called **a mono-ethnidnatic spirit.** People of this nature are content with only one ethnidnatic spirit and systematize their spiritual development only in this direction.

When a person possesses more than one ethnidnatic spirit, it is called **a multi-ethnidnatic spirit.** Man can experience several ethnidnatic spirits at intervals or in the form of simultaneous syntheses.

Dominant spirit. The people who have multiethnidnatic spirit always have dominant ethnidnatic spirit, and these ethnidnas are much stronger and more sensitive than other ethnidnas.

Ethnidna is an acronym for ethnidnatic spirit. Although a long form of the phrase is always used in this book, this word will be used a lot in our future books.

LES is the shortened form of Level of Ethnidnatic Spirit. It is a grading system used primarily by professional ethnidnatists to evaluate objects and representations. It is often used to measure the correct expression of the ethnidnatic spirit in the areas of ethnidnatic style.

The principle of hangers is considered to be one of the main principles of ethnidnatic style. It is a principle used to make ethnidnatic spirits more effective and attractive. It can be used mainly in clothing, architecture, sculpture.

The pyramid of representation is the name given to a set of systems about how a person can more accurately represent his or her own ethnidnatic spirit. The resemblance to a pyramid is related to how a person correctly establishes his inner hierarchy.

Spiritual practice correctly lists material and spiritual steps to be taken for the development of the ego. It is important to develop the ego that covers it before developing ethnidnatic spiritual practice. People who do not develop the ego properly, who only strive for the development of the ethnidnatic spirit, inevitably acquire a racist spirit or an artificial ethnidnatic spirit.

Ethnidnatic Spiritual Practice is the best way to live and develop the ethnidna you have. When the ethnidnatic spirit does not develop properly, the ego is not nourished properly, and as a result, the acquired ethnidnatic spirit becomes insignificant after a certain period.

Active and passive mudras. Although there is a concept of mudras in Buddhism and Hinduism, there is not such a notion as active and passive mudras. Ethnidnatism explains this notion as it encompasses more philosophy and spiritual practice. If a person's image of mudra needs action and activates the ethnidnatic spirit in this way, it is called active mudra. If it provides activation and balance in silence, then it is considered passive mudra.

Human ethnidnatism is the name given to the level of common spirit that remains between the ethnidnatic spirit and the ego. If ethnidna is the embodiment of the ego, human ethnidna is its lower level. The same and unchanging thing in all human beings is the spirit. Everyone has a human ethnidna. Thanks to human ethnidna, people restore peace, and even incompatible ethnidnatic spirits are bound together by this harmony.

APHORISMS BY ATASAK

I.   *The biggest factor that confuses ethnidnatic groups is the state of chaos.*
(2020)

II.   *Seek freedom inside of you, if there is no outside...*
(2020)

III.   *Man is a boundless being...*
(2020)

IV.   *Don't equate desire with being able to desire, whoever is able to desire will get it, whoever simply desires will be left back.*
(2018)

V.   *You are already dead if you don't enjoy your inner world.*
(2017)

VI.   *You run after the adornment of the material world, and if you stop running, make sure that the adornments of the material world follow you.*
(2017)

VII.   *Science is exactness based on assumptions.*
(2017)

VIII.   *If the freedom of thought is not protected in a completely positive way, it becomes negative.*
(2017)

IX. *Not the spirit, but the body takes the form of the spirit.*
(2017)

X. *Learning is a way to discovery...*
(2017)

XI. *Anxiety is nothing more than the feeling of excitement caused by negative energy.*
(2017)

XII. *Not a new phenomenon, but an unknown one, something that has always existed, worries a man.*
(2017)

TABLE OF CONTENTS

Printed in the USA
CPSIA information can be obtained
at www.ICGtesting.com
LVHW040142150224
771722LV00003B/75

9 791220 143745